VILLA DECOR

VILLA DECOR

Decidedly French and Italian Style

Betty Lou Phillips

GIBBS
P
SMITH

Gibbs Smith, Publisher
Salt Lake City

First Edition
06 05 04 03   5 4 3 2

Photographic credits on page 192

Published by
Gibbs Smith, Publisher
P.O. Box 667
Layton, Utah 84041

Orders: (1-800) 748-5439
www.gibbs-smith.com

Edited by Madge Baird
Designed and produced by Cherie Hanson
Printed and bound in Hong Kong

Library of Congress Cataloging-in-Publication Data

Phillips, Betty Lou.
Villa decor : decidedly French and Italian style / Betty Lou Phillips.— 1st ed.
p. cm.
ISBN 1-58685-174-8
1. Interior decoration—United States. 2. Interior decoration—France—Influence. 3. Interior decoration—Italy—Influence. I. Title.
NK2003 .P53 2002
747.213—dc21
2002007224

Front Jacket: "Whenever I go, I am surrounded by these beautiful objects . . . and all is Italian; not a house, not a shed, not a field that the eye can for a moment imagine to be American," Ralph Waldo Emerson once said. But only because he had not happened upon the villa featured on the cover. Although it might well be set in Italy, proudly it stands in the States with the sun streaming through arches framing the loggia. Fountain is from Le Louvre Antiques, Dallas, Texas.

Title Page: In the eighteenth century, chic French chairs came in a parade of well-documented shapes and unlikely sizes worthy of standing ovations. Making a grand entrance is a pair of Louis XIV *fauteuils* fashionably dressed in an early tapestry. Once, a chair with a high back was called a *chaire à bras*, and *fauteuils* referred to armchairs with low backs.

Facing Page: In an entrance hall with the architectural trappings of a grand *palazzo*, a *récamier* wearing a suggestive Quadrille carved velvet is rife with the romance of an earlier era. In 1805, Napoléon exiled the provocative Madame Récamier, who offered inspiration for this piece. However, after Napoléon's defeat at Waterloo in 1815, she returned to Paris and resumed her salon. On the villa wall hang an Italian mirrored niche from the eighteenth century and a nineteenth-century tapestry.

Facing Contents Page: As befitting an Italianate villa, furnishings are not only of similar visual weight but also in scale with a sumptuous space revering symmetry. Matching Italian sleigh sofas from Cache anchor the room, with chairs from the Cameron Collection settled nearby. The leather bench is from Therien & Company, San Francisco, while the coffee tabletop was once an antique iron gate. Roman baths sprayed with flowers date from the seventeenth century.

End Sheets: The 1793 inaugural flight of a hydrogen-filled balloon inspired "Le Ballon de Genosse," an original Oberkapmf factory *toile de Jouy* pattern. This historic event began at the Champs de Mars—before the Eiffel Tower was built—and ended in the village of Genosse, where townspeople attacked the balloon, believing it was an alien object. Fabric and wall covering are available from Pierre Deux stores nationwide.

Back Jacket: Once upon a time, not very many centuries ago, every courtyard in Venice had a wellhead, or wishing well, since they were the city's primary sources of water until late in the nineteenth century. Italian wellheads were crafted from a solid piece of stone, and then outfitted with relief designs that stood out from the surface.

Contents

Acknowledgements

Above all, one must not believe that beauty is a good fortune that only a few can obtain.

—*Ellen Key*

Like most books, Villa Décor was a collaborative effort. I am especially grateful to the gifted designers who allowed us to photograph their work: Roberto Agnolini, John Bobbitt, Gerrie Bremermann, Margaret Chambers, Donald Coan, Price Dixon, Sherry Hayslip, Dianne Josephs, John Kidd, Janie Petkus, Christina Phillips, Marilyn Phillips, Lynn Sears, Tony Stavish, Cecilia Talley, Clair Talley, Beau Theriot, Richard Trimble, Rebecca Turner Wiggins, Deborah Fain Walker, Liz Lank Williamson, and Warren Wyatt.

Thank you, too, to those who graciously opened the wrought-iron gates to their secluded estates, allowing us entry into their private worlds: Roberto Agnolini, Barbara and Barry Beracha, Jean Brainerd, Joan and Robert Donner, Kathleen Luby, Kelli and Christopher McGuire, George Pelletier, Sarah and Stephen Pitt, Bonnie and Bo Purvois, Pamela and Shane Reynolds, Evelyn Rucker, Sandy and Tom Rouse, Melinda and Mike Russ, Sarah and William Rutherford, Patrice and Charles Shelby, and many others.

An especially warm thank-you to the friends who kindly gave their time and energy or offered an introduction or an idea: Janet Altman, Ed Bickers, Judy Blackman, Donna Burley, Bruno de la Croix-Vaubois, Adrienne Doherty, Roblyn Herndon, Joe Lugo, Carol Seay, John Sebastian, Fannie Tapper, Jayne Taylor, Medora White, and Mike Williams.

Thank you to the most wonderful and effective public relations team an author could have: Doris Bass, Judy Blackman, Carole Lou Bruton, Jane Dunne, Linda Gibbons, Nancy O'Neill, Linda Staley, and leader Medora White.

I have true admiration and appreciation for the talented photographers with whom I worked: Dan Piassick, Emily Minton, Janet Lenzen, Alise O'Brien, and Jeffrey Millies.

Villa Décor is also the result of the unfailing interest of editor Madge Baird, whose efforts I appreciate and friendship I value.

Transporting old-world elegance to a sumptuously dressed bedroom are a desk, chair, and accessories swept from Paris's flea markets. All stand camera ready in anticipation of weekend guests. Fabled *toiles* came to the United States after the American Revolution. Popular as they are, Americans still use them more sparingly than the French. We are also more likely to mix them with solids, stripes, and checks. The key to deft blending is staying within one colorway.

Preceding Overleaf: Surely, this imperial black-and-white guest room would have been the envy of Marie Antoinette, who was known to indulge her passion for *toile*. Both wallcovering and fabric are from Pierre Deux. Pillow fabric is by LeeJofa. Headboard is from Wallner Antiques in Chicago, while swing-arm lamps were air-freighted from Besselink & Jones, London.

Introduction

Though we travel the world over to find the beautiful, we must carry it with us or we find it not.

—*Ralph Waldo Emerson*

Some things never change: We observe, we listen, we learn, yet life is full of deep mysteries. Global economies rise and fall. And like countless Americans before us, we are irresistibly drawn to the beauty of Paris with its historic monuments, ancient fountains, and towering stone façades offering a glimpse of the city's fabled past. Also igniting passions that we tend to reserve for the arts are the archeological wonders of imperial Rome, fading frescos in Florence, and, of course, Venice's decorative stonework.

Besotted, in fact, with everything in such legendary places—from the charming, shuttered villas flanked by potted plants to the shop windows filled with lengths of sumptuous hand-loomed silks—it is hardly surprising that we would find inspiration, prompting fresh ideas and hard-to-resist desires.

Little wonder, then, that we surrender to an acquired taste for furnishings with quiet French elegance and the simplicity of the sweet life, or *la dolce vita*, as the Italians say, virtuously juxtaposing various periods and styles in widely diverse, satisfying rooms that are never dull and predictable, but when revamped call attention to our *savoir-faire* and recognize the pleasures of our globe-hopping.

These days, no one says a memorable *appartement* (residential suite) has to be one style, or that a *pied-à-terre* (the convenient escape from one's principal residence) can't be open to disparate, far-flung influences. The long-standing purist look is now last century. Suddenly, mixing furnishings from different eras and the unlikeliest of places is much more chic.

Topping the sofa table is a collection of antique alabaster. Volterra is the center of alabaster carving in Italy, with quarries surrounding the Tuscan city. The Etruscans were the first to sculpt chalk-white alabaster urns, which were ideal for holding the ashes of their dead.

Preceding Overleaf: Strains of composer Claude Debussy's "Clair de Lune" waft from the ivory keys of the Playel piano, circa 1854, as other handsome French antiques—Louis XV chairs, the vintage light fixture, and an eighteenth-century *buffet à deux corps*—add to the elegant tone. Music room drapery fabric is from Great Plains; the trim is by Clarence House. The ottoman is from the Cameron Collection at George Cameron Nash, Dallas.

Taking advantage of today's creative freedom, we rely on our instincts for defining *bon goût*, gathering important *objets d'art*, glittering rock-crystal chandeliers, graceful iron gates, whatever, from assorted nations but most notably Italy and France. Conventional wisdom has it, after all, that the unerring style of these countries stems from the elegance of their people, *habitués* forever synonymous with timeless good taste, sophisticated assurance, decorative ingenuity, and startling panache. As Shakespeare sagely pointed out, "What is the city but the people?"

So it follows that, equally influenced by the Italians and the French, we justly praise the accoutrements that set their worlds apart: dramatic architecture, celebrated cultures, well-tended gardens, and strong classic interiors.

Daringly then, we fuse the very influences for which the French and Italian people are known, artfully sculpting uniquely American visions of twenty-first-century uptown living with, at best, breathtaking creativity and astonishing harmony and warmth.

Betty Lou Phillips, ASID
Author and Interior Stylist

Old World Elegance

Simplicity, carried to an extreme, becomes elegance.

—*Jon Franklin*

In the discriminating world of interior design, France and Italy have forever commanded respect, setting standards of excellence with their fine furniture, regal array of textiles, and *papiers peints*, or painted wallpapers. Also enrapturing an international roster of admirers for some years now are the treasured tapestries, distinctive porcelains, stunning crystal, and delicate embroidered linens about which the people of these nations rightly boast.

Facing Page: Impeccably crafted balconies look over a lofty *salotto*, which in Italy is where people visit. The room's generous proportions are warmed by decorative techniques—stenciling, glazing, and faux finishing—that became popular during the Italian Renaissance. In collaboration with designer John Kidd, artist Rusty Arena brought harmony to the space.

Preceding Overleaf: Architectural grandeur enhances the luxurious feeling of a villa *salotto* with a restrained color palette and impressive pieces from eras past. The well-traveled, hand-tooled leather screen, dating from the eighteenth century, arrived in Houston from Italy—following a respite at Suzanne Golden Antiques in New York. Chairs from nineteenth-century Spain wear a hand-embroidered Rentmeister chenille. The Dessin Fournier coffee table is American made.

As it happens, even proud Americans readily concede that the French and Italians have an edge when it comes to creating artful, elegant interiors with the aura of romance and glamour. For centuries, Italy was the undisputed arbiter of taste and style—deeply rooted in the region's vulnerable history of invasions by the Austrians, French, and Spanish, who each left an imprint of their customs and ways of living after claiming this picturesque land as their own.

Milan and Florence, for example, fell under the rule of France, while Sicily and Naples were ruled by Spain; Venice was controlled by Austria until the nineteenth century. From a network of duchies, principalities, and independent city-states, the Republic of Italy was created on March 17, 1861, with Turin as the capital. For political reasons, the center of government was moved to Florence in 1866, and finally Rome was declared the capital in 1871, a year after being conquered.

Distinct regional styles had emerged during the Middle Ages (1000–1450) after the Romans destroyed much of Italy's earlier Etruscan culture, whose exquisite gold and bronze metalwork was influenced by the Greeks. The Romans, too, borrowed elements from the Greeks; however, it was their own effective technological advances and skillful engineering that made it possible to span spaces with arched corridors, vaulted ceilings, and rounded domes. Since then, their influence in Europe and the West has remained indisputable.

John Notman, who emigrated from Scotland in 1831, is universally credited with introducing the Italianate villa to the United States. In 1839, he designed Riverside, a private residence in Burlington, New Jersey, that might have been transported from Tuscany. To the dismay of historic preservationists, it was razed in 1961. Nearby, however, the much-photographed Prospect mansion, built in 1851 at the center of Princeton's campus, stands in testament to the architect's love for Italy.

Indifferent to changing times, villas, *palazzi*, *châteaux*, and *hôtels particuliers* on sprawling European estates resound with the refined elegance of centuries-old furniture, expertly woven fabrics, and Aubusson carpets unfurled under aristocratic feet. Of course, not everyone lives in such imposing architectural grandeur meticulously dressed. Barely 25 percent of Parisians live in houses, while in tidy smaller French hamlets, 75 percent of the people dwell in single-family homes within a stone's throw of each other.

Intrigued by the beauty of the *fleur-de-lis,* France's heraldic symbol of unity and harmony, Dallas designer Deborah Walker incorporated the motif in a chandelier chain to complement the home's French architecture.

Facing Page: Windows bathe a stairway in light. The olive jar is an antique.

Another view of the room on page 23, this one features the antique stone chimneypiece—an ornamental structure surrounding the fireplace opening—with a patina that is impossible to reproduce. The antique tapestry, desk, and chimneypiece were all French finds.

Facing Page: Simplicity is key to a sophisticated yet no-fuss, family-friendly room. The sofa is covered in Marvic Textiles and chairs with slits in their skirts boast Brunschwig & Fils, while tape culled from Clarence House adds further interest. References to the past also abound: the bookcase, coffee table, and wine table are all antiques, unearthed during a stay in France.

This unpretentious antique, purchased in Paris, offers a less-conventional spot to stock fresh towels and keep sponges, soaps, and lotions close at hand. The master-bath floor is laid in a rhythmic pattern.

Facing Page: Soothing neutrals and an enduring passion for history give a master bedroom the layered look that usually comes with time. Night tables, lamps, and the iron bed were bought in Paris. Turning an old iron gate into a headboard was a task that fell to Potter Art Metal in Dallas. The Nancy Corzine harlequin fabric, like other fabrics in the room, required careful matching of patterns. Glowing Venetian plaster walls also were labor intensive, as one would expect.

Against gently colored textured walls stands an eighteenth-century rosewood commode that exudes a quiet richness. To create a *marqueterie* pattern, contrasting materials are set into a veneered surface.

Facing Page: Sophisticated Europeans have long had an abiding love for tapestries. In the late fifteenth century, the aristocracy used them to insulate damp walls of their *châteaux* and castles. Though America is a much younger country, we too have a passion for works of art, such as the historic French-loomed wall hanging, circa 1900. A 35-foot-wide Miró tapestry hung in the World Trade Center until destroyed on September 11, 2001.

Similarly, in scattered Italian cities, families often inhabit *palazzi* bearing their nation's storied past that have been converted into intimate, airy apartments with lofty doors opening wide onto balconies fringed with flowers. Frankly, owning palatial havens with chilly halls, flaking plaster, hefty maintenance fees, and long-ignored grounds simply does not appeal to the sensibilities of many French and Italian aristocrats, or even to those the French call the *jeunesse dorée*—the young and moneyed—a more relaxed privileged generation. They see the size of a house as less important than its furnishings and the way those pieces mirror the life within. For them, there is no signature look any more than there is one distinctive way to live. There is, however, a classic approach to space planning—guided by intelligence, awareness, and panache. It is a given that furnishings should be the best one can afford, testifying to one's impeccable taste while discreetly offering a window into one's soul.

Tellingly, then, spaces are chicly rendered works of art, exuding a passion for beauty, an intuitive sense of scale, harmony of color, and reflection of one's inner self. Marrying old-world craftsmanship with an audacious mix of treasures handed down from caring ancestors, settings look as if they've been furnished at an unhurried pace by several generations of family who had explicit ideas on style.

Massive portraits, sculpture, cherished books, and other enviable links to bygone eras holding court hundreds of years later offer the reassuring feeling of the familiar, and somehow make grand, pleasingly proportioned rooms appear even grander. It is not enough, however, for quarters to brim with prized objects displayed like museum artifacts. Ultimately, convention dictates that possessions must reveal interesting aspects of versatile lives as well as represent the culture of those exhibiting them.

As a result, humble antiques mingle graciously with more important pieces, relaxing formality and balancing the splendor of rooms. Masterfully cut and flawlessly tailored window treatments brush the

Facing Page: Traversing time zones and connecting continents, a library resplendent in oak paneling assuredly casts its own light on the world. A porcelain collection of Napoléon Bonaparte's generals rests in the nineteenth-century *bibliothéque.* Sprawled on the oak *parquet de Versailles* floor is an antique Tabriz rug, another find from the Renaissance Collection in Dallas.

In seventeenth-century France, *chinoiserie* became the rage, so it's only natural that a retrofitted *commode* with nature delicately illustrated would take center stage in a guest powder room. Aside from geometric themes, pagodas, people, and birds are common Oriental motifs. The mirror, from a Paris dealer in the Marché Biron, adds glamour.

Left: A family room pays homage to fine antiques while displaying a less assuming style than that associated with the Sun King, Louis XIV. Anchoring the room is an antique Persian Tabriz from the Renaissance Collection, Dallas. French countryside finds, including the Régence fireplace and the eighteenth-century *buffet à deux corps*, reflect the owners' worldliness.

Garnishes of French, Italian, Portuguese, and Turkish descent bestow an international flavor on a villa kitchen where copper—a natural conductor of heat—sways conveniently from a pot rack, ready to satisfy an appetite for *pain au chocolat*. With its old-world charm, the Village St.-Paul in Paris's fourth *arrondissement* is one of the best places to recapture the spirit of another era.

Preceding Overleaf: A sophisticated mix of furnishings shapes a salon with architectural presence to spare. The corbels (brackets supporting beams) are eighteenth-century Italian, as is the *pietra dura* (mosaic marble inlay) cabinet found on Via Maggio in Florence. The *console* is period Régence. Above it and across the way hang "cartoons"—renderings created before tapestries were woven. If the stories that abound are to be believed, weavers wandered from place to place, settling temporarily in the *château*, church, or monastery, where they would receive a commission after presenting detailed drawings that later served as the guide for chosen designs. The Persian rug, in the Bakhtiari pattern, is an antique from the Renaissance Collection, Dallas.

Crisscrossing the ocean shores up a breakfast room with a wave of fine antiques. Régence chairs—from the Marché aux Puces, outside Paris—are period. The set of hand-painted asparagus plates boasts the crackle finish characteristic of handmade Majolica, dating back to the thirteenth century when Italian artisans first adopted this craft from Moorish potters. The *glissant* (sliding panel) is an example of the Provençal cabinetmaker's artistry. Sliding panels—with a small tabernacle, or door, between—are designed for storing tableware without disturbing items on the buffet traditionally set beneath it. The table in the style of Louis XV is from Country French Interiors, Dallas.

To this day the eighteenth century is thought the most elegant era in European history. It was common for villas of the aristocracy to employ attendants responsible for maintaining and repairing upholstery, and textiles were woven to cover a specific piece of furniture. Here, fabrics from Scalamandré, Cowtan & Tout, and Fonthill preside over a family room where the living is easy.

Above: Nowhere is historic hand-painted furniture more popular than in Italy. A *secrétaire* cleverly outfitted with secret drawers for storing love letters and niches to hold stationery reflects the eighteenth-century practice of hand-delivering notes. The curtain fabric is from LeeJofa.

Preceding Overleaf: Fashionably exposed beams and imported Portuguese tile garnish a country kitchen stocked with stained, glazed, and dry-brushed cabinets. The chandelier is from Ironies in Berkeley, California. The *faïence* was culled from flea markets.

Below: Galatians 5:22 offers a gentle reminder that Spirit is love, joy, peace, patience, kindness, goodness, faithfulness, gentleness, and self-control.

floor with soft braid or fringe trimming drizzled from pencil-thin piped edging. A stream of perfectly matched stripes, florals, and storied *toiles* affectionately hug upholstery, though in less dressy spaces seamstress tucks often nestle amid shapely slipcovers as unassuming seagrass offhandedly blankets well-traveled floors.

Everywhere you look there are blooms of cascading flowers suiting the spirit of striking, interestingly textured rooms. With neither the French nor the Italians inclined to compromise their standards, Porthault and Frette linens—fashioned of Egyptian cotton in France and Italy, respectively—are spritzed with scented water, making beds romantically inviting. *En suite*, enough thick, fluffy towels to comfortably stock Paris's legendary Hôtel Ritz or the princely sixteenth-century Villa d'Este, which sits on the banks of Italy's Lake Como outside Milan, soak up centuries of history.

Traditional Italian kitchens appear tidy, orderly, and clutter-free. With a place for everything and everything in its place when not in use, spring-latched cupboard doors mask precisely stacked molds, various-sized mixing bowls, colanders, and metal cauldrons. Fruits and vegetables not requiring refrigeration sit in small metal boxes on balconies until called upon to express regional preferences.

Meanwhile, practicality holds sway in French kitchens, where baskets for storing crusty breads and scores of copper pots in graduating sizes crowd ceilings, proudly hanging out within easy reach on pot racks, or *crémaillères*, which are almost as integral in the French kitchen as cross-timbers and weathered walls.

A medieval *manoir* in the Pays d'Auge région—a verdant province of Normandy—inspired a timber and brick dwelling built recently in the States. Like the typical Norman roofline, this one is steeply pitched, not only making the house aesthetically charming but also facilitating drainage when it rains. The Cuban mahogany front door once graced a school in England.

Facing Page: An earthy palette, vintage leather chairs, and tattered pieces of history create an inviting sitting room off the kitchen where friends may gather to keep the cook company. Most often, however, it is the perfect spot to savor an early morning *café au lait à deux* and peruse the morning papers, then discuss world issues at the end of the day. In seventeenth-century Spain, the carved wooden shield hung in the back of a church; its coat of arms represented three families serving as protectors and benefactors.

Most kitchens in France do not have upper cabinets. Rather, open shelving allows ready access to *la batterie de cuisine*—pitchers, platters, goblets, tureens, and any other items needed. Countertops burst with dozens of utensils for every imaginable purpose, while colorful *faïence* (pottery with luminous glazes), heavy Continental-size flatware, and bowls of apples garnish tables set on terra-cotta tile betraying its age.

In contrast, when the Mediterranean sun sinks into the horizon, dining rooms sparkle like diamonds—impeccably set—as glistening silver, breathtaking crystal, and a regal mix of delicate china showcase culinary talents.

For serious cooks, cuisine is more than a means to satisfy the pangs of hunger; it is rather a theatrical production, inventively propped, perfectly staged, and, most importantly, designed to elicit applause. Accordingly, candlelight swirls over flavors and aromas needing little introduction, highlighting dramatically the link between how food looks and the architectural manner in which it is presented.

In France, the expression *epater le bourgeois* means "to astonish them"—and the French have more than risen to the challenge of bracing occasions with this attitude. Whether a casual breakfast, a picnic lunch, an afternoon tea or a leisurely dinner *à deux*, nothing escapes attention. Service plates are noticeably liberal in size, goblets gleam, and linens appear crisp, having been painstakingly pressed. Masses of the same cut flower, assembled with a French touch—tightly packed and equal in height—look obligingly unarranged.

Old-world opulence reigns in an entrance hall whose intricately hand-painted ceiling was inspired by the chapel in Le Lude, the imposing thirteenth-century *château* standing on an elevated bank of the Loire, France's longest river. Artist Dan Pedigo lives in Dallas, Texas.

Facing Page: Staking claim to the air space over the great room is an eighteenth-century bronze Russian chandelier thought to have hung in a Kremlin church. Some say the antique August Forster piano, from East Germany, is the finest piano made. It was bought in Paris after the fall of the Berlin Wall. The nineteenth-century French Empire breakfront is rosewood and in keeping with the space's grand proportions. Both paintings are by Frenchman Edouard Cortes (1882–1969).

Indeed, the French fervor for fine food is expected to start early. In France's *école maternelle*, three-year-olds bake pies. For one week each year, the French also use their gastronomic know-how to teach their children how to appreciate fine food and wine.

Leaving little to chance, some three thousand chefs sweep through classrooms throughout the country, talking about taste, flavor, and discussing the anatomy of the tongue before taking students on a cook's tour of outdoor markets where they learn to carefully choose the pick of the crop.

With a lot to learn about what to do, and what not to do, no child's education is considered complete without help in demystifying fine dining. Predictably, then, chefs stir up regional dishes masterminded by fancy restaurants that have garnered Michelin stars, the hospitality industry's most coveted honor. By revealing secrets of their country's culinary excellence, the art of French living is passed from one generation to another.

A dining room layered in French history offers a visual feast, tempting guests with treasures holding closely guarded secrets. Both the antique velvet screen and the vintage table runners are from The Mews, Dallas. Curtain fabric is by Randolph & Hein; trim is Schumacher. Dining tables were uncommon until the time of Louis XVI.

Preceding Overleaf: Handsome furnishings honor Louis XV. Family room chairs are robed in Pindler & Pindler while curtains and sofas are clad in LeeJofa, one of America's oldest fabric houses, established in 1832. The skirted table is draped in vintage Fortuny. Mariano Fortuny (1871–1949) was born in Granada, Spain. He studied chemistry in Germany and sculpture with Rodin in Paris before starting the impressive design house.

Serving Suggestions

*Since one cannot be universal and know
everything there is to know about everything,
one must know a little about everything.*
—Blaise Pascal

No tasteful dinner party is complete without polished fine silver, sparkling crystal, oversized linen napkins, and a striking mix of resplendent china patterns dispatched from overseas, not to mention place cards and a pianist. But when fittingly attentive waiters aren't available to deliver flutes of Veuve Clicquot, *la grande dame of champagnes*, on silver trays to guests with an air of power, the right serving piece can add a bit more importance to any setting. Here are some choices that are most tempting:

Bombé: A style of *commode.* The word itself in French means "blown out," and the earliest *commode*—with bulging front and plumped sides—was introduced in the Régence period. However, it was equally fashionable during the rococo period and nowadays is just as popular. The most valuable pieces do not have a dividing rail or strip between the upper and lower drawers.

A delectable first course.

Facing Page: If one's home is his or her castle, should not the table appear regally garbed in linens by Pratesi—with a gold-rimmed Rosenthal china pattern and Strasbourg sterling by Gorham enhancing its beauty? The French Baccarat crystal pattern "Harcourt," designed specifically for Pope Pius XII, is still used at the Vatican and only recently became available in the United States. Turn-of-the-twentieth-century dining chairs, made in Italy, once belonged to the late William Randolph Hearst. The glossy wall finish, called French polish, complements the aura of the *manoir.*

Buffet: A sideboard or cupboard whose doors mask shelves satisfying the need for storage space. In France, a buffet forty to forty-two inches tall is most prized, even though the French, as a people, are rather short. Yet ease is not a priority. Instead, style is.

Buffet à deux corps: A cupboard in two pieces with the lower section somewhat wider than the upper piece.

Bureau commode: A large writing table with drawers, dating back to the era of Louis XIV.

A finely carved Louis XV walnut buffet, circa 1860, from French Country Interiors, Dallas, has a place of honor beneath prized old German doors, which open to the kitchen. Showing obvious signs of age are Portuguese chairs with lighthearted vintage trim. They are from Nick Brock Antiques, Dallas.

Facing Page: To escape from today's fast lane, a gathering place demands space neither too formal nor fancy, relaxed fabrics, and oversized sofas where family and friends can share concerns as well as laughs. The earthtone palette is drawn from the nineteenth-century Oushak area rug, an Oriental rug of Turkish origin, geometric in design with a wide border.

Bureau plat: *Bureau* is the French word for desk. A rectangular, flat-topped writing table covered in leather. Most have three drawers.

Commode: A low, flat-topped chest of drawers or cabinet that was the rage of eighteenth-century France, and remains an important piece of furniture today.

Commode desserte: A sideboard intended for storing china, with center cabinet flanked by open shelves.

Console: French for "bracket." Supported by brackets, two legs, or flat-topped ornamental S-shaped scrolls, it is a table or a shelf that juts from a wall.

Console d'applique: A *console* table that stands against a wall.

Console de milieu: A large, free-standing table.

Console desserte: A small serving table.

Console servante: A marble-topped serving table with a shelf, similar to the *console desserte* and *commode desserte*, launched during Louis XVI's time.

Console table: A shelf-like table supported by S-shaped *caryatid* (sculptured female figure) brackets or two legs. Rooted in eighteenth-century France and England, it was also known as a pier table.

Crédence: A sideboard or serving table with drawers for storing tablecloths, napkins, and silver, and with doors especially useful for concealing dishes and glasses. The word itself comes from the Latin *credere*, meaning "to believe," and the earliest piece dates back to the Gothic period (1300–1500), when it was inspired by a religious chest mounted on a stand. In Italy, this same piece is called a *credenza*.

Demilune: A semicircular or half-moon *console*, generally one of a pair set against opposite walls until called into service. Since it is easily moved, it can be fitted against opposite ends of a rectangular dining table, thus creating an oval table capable of catering to a larger group.

Desserte: A small serving table or sideboard with one or more tiered shelves, introduced during the reign of Louis XVI.

Enfilade: A low, provincial buffet with four or more cupboard doors, providing ample storage and making it invaluable in the country home. Also, the French word for a set or suite of rooms, literally a row.

As if confirming its versatility, the coveted Louis XV buffet stores china, silver, and linens, while the top is open to serving after-dinner coffee and sweets that look as if they came from the *patisseries* of Paris. Further indulging sophisticated tastes, lush silk taffeta—piped with an Ellen Holt trim—hang at the dining room window.

Facing Page: An artfully fashioned dining room brims with culture and charm, as France, Italy, and the United States each have their say, thanks to antique wood pieces from Provence, pottery hand-painted in Tuscany, and Ralph Lauren Home crystal and flatware. Walls sing the praises of Venetian plaster. Dressing Louis XV chair backs is fabric from Nancy Corzine, Los Angeles; fronts and seats wear supple leather.

Hutch: From the Old French *huche*, meaning bin or chest. A cabinet or cupboard with open shelving, or shelves flanked by doors, that rests upon a buffet.

Ménagère: A low cabinet with open shelves equipped with racks and guardrails, making it ideal for storing crockery. Also called a *vaisselier*.

Pier table: A *console* table originally intended for the area, or pier, between two windows.

Vaisselier: A cabinet or hutch fashioned during the reign of Louis XIV in Lorraine, France, an established center for manufacturing porcelain, where wealthy landholders yearned for a piece of furniture appropriate for displaying fine china. Less well known is the *vaisselier's* more regal cousin, the *grand vaisselier*, developed in nearby Bresse for holding homemade liqueurs.

Inarguably, this kitchen owes a heaping portion of its allure to the quilted copper backsplash and custom hardware by Brad Oldham, Dallas. But like our French and Italian cousins, we also prize copper cookware, which efficiently handles routine tasks by heating quickly and evenly at low temperatures, then cooling quickly too.

Facing Page: With the magnetic charm of Normandy, a morning room shares its architectural grandeur and reveals the undulating woodlands surrounding it. Raised paneled walls are pegged with black walnut, while the Napoléon III table is lauded for its book-matched burled walnut top. The antique terra-cotta tile once covered the roof of a South of France *château;* barrel tile then topped it—long before being ferried to the Ann Sacks Collection, where it was sidemarked for this home.

New World Excellence

To look at a thing is very

different from seeing a thing.

One does not see anything

until one sees its beauty.

—*Oscar Wilde*

Paying homage to those who have, by example, taught us about glamour, grace, and unerring taste, we let the people of France and Italy establish the standard of beauty by which our rooms are judged. But neither their boundless self-assurance nor their unshakable stylistic authority takes a toll on our creative energy.

Facing Page: A niche in the master bathroom owes its playfulness to the leopard lounging on the daybed. Though zebra, giraffe, and cheetah prints take refuge on both sides of the Atlantic, it is leopard that the French think is *très* cool. The Stroheim & Romann curtain also helps capture a look that is chic. Fabric from Kravet camouflages the wall.

Preceding Overleaf: In a villa with soaring ceilings, massive walls, lavish architectural detailing, and extraordinary art, guests might well imagine themselves at a dinner honoring visiting dignitaries. The table is set with Baccarat crystal, Bernardaud china, and flatware from the Italian house of Buccellati, known the world over. The painted and gilded dining chairs are by Nancy Corzine.

Quite the contrary: It is not just that both the French and Italians have unparalleled style that can't be copied, however hard we try. Nor is it even that we wish to broadcast what some might mistake as affluence any more than failed ambitions. Instead, it is that we pride ourselves on fashioning posh yet welcoming spaces in a beguiling way and, not incidentally, on being admired for steering away from safe harbors and skirting well-charted paths.

What better time than now, after all, to show that the American flag's broad stripes and bright stars represent freedom, to say nothing of the indisputable right to lend a global look to any interior?

Putting our diplomatic skills to the test, we boldly fuse the unbreakable spirit of America with the heightened sophistication of Europe to imbue our houses with a style suggesting our artistry, love of life, desire for comfort and considerable beauty.

What finer place to wash away the cares of the day than in a French Empire tub? It is, of course, all-important fixtures and fittings that conspire to make a world of difference in any bathroom. The freestanding tub dating from the nineteenth century springs from Water Monopoly in London, England, restorers of antique bathroom fixtures.

Facing Page: Summing up all that is French, a bedroom in *le style Provençal* might very well be set in a farmhouse, or *mas,* in the South of France. Both the *toile* and stripe are from Schumacher. In its former life the lamp was an old oil lantern; Van Horn & Hayward in Houston wired it and then topped it with a custom shade.

An antique daybed with lavish scrollwork is outfitted in vintage fabrics from a variety of places. Daybeds—resembling rustic cot-sized beds with footboards on both ends—first appeared in American homes at the beginning of the twentieth century. The table holding pears is an antique.

Facing Page: European antiques hugging countertops deliver generous helpings of charm to a St. Louis, Missouri, kitchen suited to the impeccable taste of a cook who revels in creating innovative dishes that are as pleasing to the eye as to the palate.

Well before the September 11, 2001, terrorist attacks on the United States, we frowned on the inexcusably opulent and shunned pretension. Wisdom also discouraged the flaunting of swank extravagances and, for that matter, thinking about the display of wealth as a passport to respectability.

Plainly, mellowed patterned rugs, chandeliers bearing dust, painted pieces having weathered years of loving wear, and towering *armoires* made in scattered provincial towns for the day's minor nobility appeal to our modern sensibility. Apart from adding luster, they create the feeling of intimacy in generously proportioned spaces where seating is artfully arranged to encourage serious discussions about the predicament in the Middle East, or talk about issues that are personal.

By our own admission, we have a penchant for vintage pillows tucked snugly in the embrace of plump upholstery, and for salvaged handcrafted locks and hinges respecting the period of the house. Never mind haughty European acquisitions snapped up at the famed Marché aux Puces de Saint-Ouen, the vast weekend flea market on the outskirts of Paris, or gathered in Parma, Italy—where dealers serve as beacons of hope for making Italian rooms look Italian. Still, when it comes to that which strikes our fancy, beauty matters more to us than provenance, or the history of a piece—and quality is key.

The belief that guest quarters should be no less stylish than the master bedroom opens the door to a room that is not merely a place to sleep. Swathes of beautiful fabrics add drama to the Su-Su III carriage canopy from The Farmhouse Collection; lamps on night tables are by Festoné. At the foot of the bed rests a vintage trunk from Ireland that not only reminds us that "getting there" was once half the fun, but also doubles as a luggage stand. The French writing desk dates from 1880. Dallasite Jane Shook artfully stenciled the walls.

Affection for France travels into another guest room where a visiting dignitary might rest easy. Making a world of difference are a bed from Amy Howard and a chandelier by Murray's Iron Works. The marble-topped chest from Inessa Stewart Antiques and an antique mirror from the Whimsey Shoppe, both in Dallas, add to the allure.

Owning a hand-painted Italian piece links us to the Italian people, not to mention letting us share that which makes their life sweeter. A handsome circa-1860 chest, whose timeworn finish and exuberant carving make it easy to distinguish from later pieces, occupies a prime spot in an entrance hall. Furniture painting began in Italy around 1300 and has long been a point of national pride.

Facing Page: Light dances under the arches framing a villa hall.

Sweeping aside any misgivings, lest we not see anything as tempting again, we juxtapose hand-painted Italian daybeds, hand-loomed Portuguese needlepoint rugs, carved French mirrors, and Swedish corner cupboards with unevenly worn paint, not to mention discarded German trunks privy to secrets sheltered for centuries. All mix amicably with international goods already in place, including hand-blown vases from the Venetian island of Murano, heavy silver candlesticks discovered in England, maps unearthed in the Louvre museum gift shop, and folding screens from the Far East, that hark back to a love for *chinoiserie*, or decorative Chinese motifs.

This is not to suggest that spaces stray toward the fussy or the cluttered in the manner of Versailles. While furnishings vary widely from one *bonne adresse* to another—thanks largely to each having its own artistic bent—mostly we adhere to Ludwig Mies van der Rohe's long-standing "less is more" school of design, meaning there need not be something in every corner or filling every inch.

This Italian limestone floor is fitted with terra-cotta pickets.

To be sure, we long ago recognized that one liberally scaled treasure could, with few exceptions, make a stronger statement than many fragile trinkets. Yet, if anything, it is unexpected expressions of care that elicit admiring glances from those who come to call, leaving little doubt they find our attention to detail remarkable.

Even in homes stocked with all the twenty-first-century accoutrements of a new resort—counting home theaters with screens to rival the multiplex—walls are plastered in labor-intensive finishes that create time-worn backdrops for meticulously constructed window treatments duly adorned with fringe, gimp, or braid. Soft yet perfect folds tumble from iron rods hailing the light, as interlining protects draperies from fading,

Gracefully curved stairs sculpted out of French limestone lead from a first-floor hall to the *piano nobile*. The French chest, circa 1860, was found at Brian Stringer Antiques, while the *trumeau*, dated 1885, is from Area; both companies are in Houston. The whimsical crystal and bronze light fixtures came from Suzanne Golden Antiques in New York City.

and more conspicuously, adds telltale weight necessary for demure billowing. Left unlined, curtains hang in a more casual fashion. For the most part, however, draperies veer away from elaborate valances, swags, and other over-the-top treatments that invariably are more suited to a crown prince's glitzy marble palace than a gracious villa.

Pewter hardware reminds us of a simpler way of life a century ago. Dallas artisan Brad Oldham designs and manufactures French-style knobs, levers, pulls and elevator dials that are used in homes from California to Texas to New York.

Facing Page: In a niche outside the powder room sits a cabinet filled with everything a guest might need, including a gorgeous Sherle Wagner sink. Towels are from Waterworks; the accessories are from Lovers Lane Antiques, Dallas.

Meters of relaxed linen expertly woven in the textile epicenter of Lyon, France, veil the weary drawers of eighteenth-century *commodes* (chests with drawers), where ladies who lunch leave their Louis Vuitton, Chanel, Hermès, Prada, and Gucci handbags. Bolts of silk taffeta—hand-loomed in northern Italy—meanwhile envelop the aging shelves of antique *armoires*, lengthening the life of bedding by undercutting their ability to snag pricey sheets, blankets, and duvets.

For upholstery, we select jacquards, damasks, chenilles, and velvets in various weights and breathtaking hues without trading in our individuality. Natural linens with selvage borders place a mosaic of possibilities at our disposal, such as rescuing sofas and chairs from austerity with floor-sweeping bands. No matter if the idea is not quite original.

Internationally recognized oil paintings from the eighteenth, nineteenth and early twentieth century—the *belle époque*, or beautiful age that ended abruptly in 1914—generally are the preferred choice

of those who have an obsession for art. But congenial mixes of equally impressive engravings, etchings, and lithographs also congregate on walls while interest in acquiring photography increases as well. As expected, some works of art stand propped above masonry fireplaces in true French fashion, while faded Aubusson, Savonnerie, and/or Oushak antique rugs—which not only are notoriously hard to come by but also provide more than a modicum of pleasure—swathe hardwood floors.

Prompted by Italians who flirt with bargains but remain faithful to the finest furniture and linens they can afford, we purchase what we really want, or do without when what is affordable and what is desirable appear far apart. Like generations of Europeans before us, we share a passion for quality craftsmanship graced with the patina of age but also value practicality. Then again, we possess a yen for uncommon beauty, obtainable, of course, for the right price.

The colors of the French and the Italian countryside to which we have taken a liking echo inside homes, making spaces appear larger or smaller than they are. Invariably, rich, deep hues render rooms snug and intimate, while softer, less saturated ones foster a sense of space. Subtly, color raises ceilings, lengthens walls, highlights architectural details, and diminishes structural flaws, not to mention sways our moods, arouses our senses, revives our souls, and gives us new appreciation for our homes.

The French have long inspired American chefs, even if some of us have not yet matched their talents. But the splendor of Stateside kitchens often puts those abroad to shame. Here, innovatively designed, silver-plated copper cabinets—custom built by the Lonestar Range Hood Company, Houston—add to the glamour of a fine French home. Open shelves put necessities within easy reach, while the Dacor commercial range bespeaks good taste.

Restoring peace of mind comes easy in the comfort of this sumptuous Summer Hill *chaise*. In eighteenth-century France the *chaise* was neither a settee nor a daybed but somewhere in between—an elongated, low *bergère* with a feather mattress, cushions, and rounded cylindrical pillows at each end.

Facing Page: Much like the French, we lavish extraordinary attention on our beds with sensuous linens, goose-down duvets, and layers of pillows. Although bed hangings no longer must fend off drafts in poorly heated rooms, they still summon images of splendor, especially when Rogers & Goffigon Ltd. and Brunschwig & Fils textiles are fabricated by Gulf Draperies in Houston. In the era of Louis XV, each bedroom had its own *garde-robe,* or dressing room, and a *boudoir* that offered a quiet spot to get away alone or, if one so chose, to receive and entertain guests.

With its classic, aristocratic good looks, a gracious room begs for a *coterie* of close friends eager to share interests while basking in the beauty of glistening silver, a Dennis & Leen chandelier, and breathtaking de Gournay silk wallcovering produced in England. The dining room was not commonplace in American homes until the mid-nineteenth century.

An appreciation for the old, the unusual, the unexpected, and the unique lead the way to a powder room that is classically French. In the fourteenth century, it was believed that mirrors held magic powers; to keep production methods secret, the Venetians threatened imprisonment and death; yet, by 1665 French mirrors began outshining those from Venice. The Josephine Zapata wallcovering is available through the Gerald Hargett Showroom, Houston. The frosted-glass sink is by Elegant Additions, also in Houston.

Below: It is only natural for haute couture curtains fit for a Paris runway or the cover of a major fashion magazine to catch the eye. Finely pleated silk shantung from Shalimar Creations, Houston, is accompanied by tassel-fringed edging from Kenneth Meyer, San Francisco. The Nile chair is by Michael Taylor Designs, Los Angeles, while the antique pillow was found at Lewis & Maese, Houston. Neiman Marcus stores carry the Jay Strongwater picture frames shown here.

Judging from the look of areas, we take at its word the old French adage, "A white wall is the fool's paper," mixing pigment in Venetian plaster—lately an ubiquitous favorite—and applying it exceedingly thin before waxing walls to a rich finish. Not that blinding, bright white would be our choice anyway: perceived as lacking sophistication, it fails to win approval even for door and window trim, apparently. By comparison, dove, ivory, parchment, and champagne—alluring tints borrowed from eighteenth-century silks—are still popular centuries later.

In well-tended gardens, heroic statuary shaded by trees stands guard over other noble ornaments. Antique fountains quietly spray arcs of water, moss-covered *jardinières* burst with foliage, and weathered park benches along with old iron tables and chairs not only present *al fresco*—the Italian phrase for "in the open air"—dining at its best, but also offer coveted spots for youngsters playing hide-and-seek away from streets and pebble-lined driveways.

To our delight, we have mastered the fabled French way of melding the past with the present so that each is seen in the best possible light, as well as the uncanny Italian knack of linking rooms effortlessly with patterns and palettes without detracting from the furnishings or *objets d'art*. But sometime late in the twentieth century, a new confidence emerged among us, helping us envision a chic way of in-town living that was no longer in awe of

At the far end of the great room stands an early-eighteenth-century Louis XV walnut commode with impressive bronze mounts. It has a place of honor beneath *Porte St. Martin* by Frenchman Antoine Blanchard (1910–88), who found the streets of Paris endlessly fascinating.

Facing Page: Majestically scaled plump sofas—covered in Christopher Norman chenille—and a subtle palette imparts a look that is both striking and chic. But it is the masterfully carved stone chimneypiece that commands attention. On its mantel rest nineteenth-century French urns. A Dennis & Leen shaped *chinoiserie* tray table hovers between the sofas.

Hand-painted sundials are often seen on the sides of stately manor houses, or *bastides,* as they are called in France. But here, the sun itself—painted by David Manning of Evanston, Illinois—shines down on a spacious morning room. Making it tempting to disagree with the old adage "There's nothing new under the sun" is a chandelier from Ironware International, which casts soft light. The French buffet dating from the nineteenth century is from Galleria, in Chicago.

Facing Page: The past and the present meet in a French drawing room. The fireplace fender, vase, and painting are all antique. Paneling dispatched from Oxfordshire, England, serves as the backdrop for a finely crafted *chinoiserie* chest from John Widdicomb Furniture. The appealing area rug arrived via Minasian Rugs, a favorite destination for Janie Petkus and other Chicago designers. The Marge Carson settee wears Beacon Hill fabric.

It's a jungle in there, a room where grandsons go wild over the monkeys and a giraffe handcrafted by Steiff, the German toy company that has been putting a button in one ear for more than one hundred years. Meanwhile, the sisal carpeting from Stark and the coarse Madagascar cloth wallcovering by Summer Hill pay homage to Malagasies weavers who live on that mysterious island in the Indian Ocean, off the southeast coast of Africa, where pirate Captain Kidd once flourished.

Preceding Overleaf: A screening room draws rave reviews with Valentino chairs covered in European leather. They were custom built in Germany by Cinema Tech Seating. *Casablanca,* with Ingrid Bergman and Humphrey Bogart, ranks as the most romantic movie of all time, according to the American Film Institute.

Pages 82—83: Capturing the signature artistry for which the French are known is an impeccably furnished retreat. Everything—from the iron daybed and swing arm lamp to the classical *toile*—speaks of Chicago designer Tony Stavish's attention to detail.

A chandelier gives this room added pizzazz.

Left: A young girl's bedroom is a world unto itself—fashioned no less stylishly than other rooms in the house. Charming Anna French wallcovering sets the palette, while trims and scalloping make for an even prettier place. The white *piqué*—French for quilted—gracing the table skirt, shades, and blanket cover is by Summer Hill. Accessories are from Room Service, Dallas.

Below: While the rest of the house hangs onto the spirit of the Old World, playful saturated colors reflect new-world thinking in a young girl's bathroom.

"...Such stuff as dreams are made on," Shakespeare once said, as if he looked around this young girl's room. The chic and comfy bedding tucked into this niche is also the perfect place to curl up with a book. The sheer is by Ralph Lauren. Most other fabrics are from Boussac of France.

Like the bedroom opposite, the bath is awash in upbeat shades of green and blue. The small check is from Cowtan & Tout.

The French *joie de vivre* can be gleaned from guest beds wearing a Quadrille *toile*. *Toiles de Jouy* originated in the mid-eighteenth century at the Oberkampf factory in the French town of Jouy-en-Josas, near Versailles. Monochrome prints, usually red or blue on white cotton or muslin ground, depicted pastoral and mythological scenes. Later, *toiles* celebrated current events.

Europe but inimitably American, replete with possibilities as regal as any abroad.

Paying little heed to the fleeting decorating trend of the moment—knowing, of course, any craze could become *passé* quickly—or even proclaiming undying affection for the single-minded style of a long-dead king to show the same restraint, we grew to be above all that. With keen eyes and a view of the world broadened beyond America, we set out on a foreign course, bulging with treasures to carefully consider.

Politely put, nowadays, a single period and genre befitting a Parisian flat appears almost defiantly dated, however well crafted.

Amid strong, stately architecture with requisite soaring ceilings, imposing stone fireplaces, generously chiseled moldings, oak *parquet de Versailles* floors, and *boiserie*, or exquisitely carved paneling, it is disparate furnishings, all with their own centuries-long résumés, that produce a distinctive look.

Indeed, our *forte* is putting a cosmopolitan spin on settings sated with riches dispatched from assorted corners of the world—sometimes without leaving the States—for they are suggestive of our personalities and forward-looking way of life.

High-Minded French

Style is the perfection

of a point of view.

—*Richard Eberhart*

There's no denying that French country has dressed itself up since Louis XIII ascended the throne in 1610. Where rough-hewn furnishings tinged with the *nostalgie* of the early seventeenth century once held sway, these days grace and glamour reflect in settings with a bit more flair, attesting to the way we live and entertain. Which is to say that the appearance of French country, echoing the furniture, fabrics, and accessories linked with the *région* of Provence, has changed over the years.

Of course, there will always be aficionados dutifully faithful to the style of Louis XIII set in a world far simpler. But on this side of the Atlantic, it seems most Americans have forsaken such Provençal clichés as hand-made rag rugs, dried bouquets, farm animals, and pillows with home-spun sayings in favor of less subtle elegance.

Facing Page: Praiseworthy wines flow in a candlelit tasting room intended for entertaining. Framing the space—built into the hollow of a rock—are embossed leather chairs still enjoying a life of privilege, plus an antique Empire table dressed in cut velvet.

Preceding Overleaf: Hidden lighting meanders like the Yangtze River over a collection of ancient leatherbound books in a two-story library, glazed Chinese red. As the dramatic spiral staircase rises to the gallery, Louis XIV reigns over a magnificent Louis XV *bureau-plat*, circa 1820, with a hand-tooled leather top and exuberant figural-bronze mounts. Equally impressive are flowers inlaid into the cross hatching.

While France has cut its work week to thirty-five hours, changed its presidential term from seven to five years, given women parity on ballots, let citizens from other European Union countries vote and run for office, and even created a type of marriage that can be dissolved on three months' notice, Americans have boldly shored up defenses in a war against terrorism, attacked domestic issues, and knowingly or not, unceremoniously fashioned an image of French country that is distinct from the French. For a while now, in fact, French country has been a widely accepted catchall term for furnishings alluring and enduring, in step with the twenty-first century here in the States.

Admittedly, blending stylistic elements from different countries produces settings that sometime outdazzle those of our oldest allies, raising some eyebrows in France, where critics contend we take a more showy approach to country décor. What passes for French country in the United States, they say tactfully, bears only a fleeting similarity to *le style Provençal*, grounded in simplicity. In truth, it *is* safe to assume that stateside rooms boast fabrics and furnishings the people of Provence would scarcely think of using.

Fulfilling visions in costly high-rises with luxurious square footage, two-story villas with mansard roofs and dormer windows, as well as houses more upscale than their modest looks imply is a redefined treasury of refined furnishings laced with ties to Italy and the Far East, but drawn mostly from a blur of styles descending from France's kings.

It is inarguable that four French monarchs—with ascending Roman numerals affixed to the name Louis—shaped the taste of their day with expertly crafted *commodes* culled from the finest *ébénistes* (cabinetmakers who specialized in *marqueterie*) and chairs, *consoles*, and *coiffeuses* (dressing tables) built by highly skilled *menuisiers* (joiners who made furniture out of solid wood). Common characteristics set apart the pieces from earlier to later eras. This is not to imply that any one desk or *armoire* necessarily displayed all traits, or that any one site was its final resting place. Tellingly, in fact, the French and Italian words for furniture—*mobilier* and *mobilia*—literally mean movable. Bolstered by large

Swathing a Stateside dining room in glamour are *boiseries,* or exquisitely carved panels that once adorned a magnificent French *château.* Skillfully painted oils on canvas—original to the sections—give rise to gracious living as guests and the home's owners alike savor their old-world splendor.

staffs, a number of royal residences at their disposal, and thoughts of their own comfort, French monarchs moved restlessly with the seasons from one sumptuous dwelling to another, crossing the River Seine with an inventory of imperial trappings that ranged from staggering to modest.

Once a series of civil wars known as the Wars of Religion or the Huguenot Wars (1562–98) were victoriously put behind him, Henry IV (1553–1610) looked to foster France's independence by reducing the need for costly imports and encouraging talented artisans from Italy and the Low Countries to set up workshops in the cavernous Grand Galerie of the Louvre, which had been transformed during the reign of Francis I from a fortress into a Renaissance palace. Loosening restrictions, the king granted permission for a brigade of leading metalsmiths, clockmakers, engravers, weavers, and others to work for private patrons as well as the court, and authorized them to train apprentices, too.

Since Louis XIII was only nine years old when his father, Henry IV, was assassinated in 1610, his mother, queen Marie de Médici, was appointed *régent*, or temporary governor of France. With obsessive ties to Italy and without any constraints, she boldly reversed policies set by her late husband, then ominously depleted a carefully amassed treasury with her astounding extravagance, including the purchase of exuberant Italian Renaissance art.

Storyboards depicting various stages of winemaking adorn the front panels of a twentieth-century tap room bar. On the back bar is a cut-to-clear carved glass mirror of the Eiffel Tower, Paris's best-known monument, built for the Exposition Universelle of 1899.

An important William IV four-fold, double-sided screen, bought at auction, lends drama and interest to a New Orleans dining room. Each panel is adorned with four paintings—some French scenes, some not—all by artist James Digman Wingfield, a member of the Royal Academy.

Furniture design, however, showed more restraint. Craftsmen built primitive, somewhat plain, *armoires* studded with somber geometric carvings, primarily diamonds and discs. Most were fabricated from oak or walnut, though many of the more soulful armoires were sculpted in supple pine.

Massive boxy chairs had bun feet and spiral or bead turned legs with *stretchers* joining the legs in an X or figure eight. Elaborately embossed Cordovan leather, velvet, damask, and tapestry needlework covered seats that were frequently glossed with fringe.

An eighteenth-century *blackamoor*—a decorative statue usually gaudily clad in oriental wear—keeps watch over a dining room. The sophisticated silk curtain fringe is custom from Smith & Brighty, London.

No different than in the time of ancient Egyptians, beds were the ultimate symbols of wealth; however, they fell into the domain of the upholsterer rather than the furniture maker, since frames were rarely carved. Bed hangings hid simple bedposts, offered privacy, and protected against cross drafts. Mattresses were stuffed with straw, leaves, and pine needles. There were no box springs; instead, a wooden frame supported a platform of planks.

To escape the stuffy, stifling formality framing life at the Louvre and a litany of ceremonial duties, Louis XIII and his wife, Anne of Austria, fled the French capital in 1624. In the serene forests of Versailles, fourteen miles southwest of Paris, the king built a modest retreat where he could indulge in hunting, his favorite sport.

But his son Louis XIV had grander visions for Versailles when he became king in 1661 at age twenty-three. Impulsively, he turned the hunting lodge built by his father into the most awe-inspiring *château* in Europe; next he turned his attention outdoors. With help from André Le Nôtre, the most acclaimed French gardener, land less than perfectly suited to plantings was leveled, drained, and shaped into a lavish horticultural fashion show, opulently garbed in 460 fountains that are still working today, trees imported from around the world, formal avenues of elaborate length, ornamental canals, stone statuary, and landscaped gardens more beautiful than those in Italy.

In pursuit of the most regal palace on earth, the Sun King and his chief architect, Louis Le Vau, created a series of lofty, almost ceremonial spaces designed especially for sleeping, eating, and socializing. *Chambres* (bedrooms), *antichambres* (salons), *garde-robes* (dressing rooms), and *cabinets* (studies) layered in overwhelming splendor fueled a taste for grandeur at every turn.

Along the way, motifs were pieced together from architecture, flora, fauna, and the instruments of war. The same attention-grabbing fabric bedecked curtains and upholstery while clinging insistently to padded walls, which, in fact, helped filter the damp, misty cold that often settled over the town. Yet for all the apparent affluence at the palace, only Louis XIV had the use of a proper bathroom with running water.

In keeping with royal demands, the king's *maître ébéniste* (chief cabinetmaker), André-Charles Boulle (1642–1732), laboriously fashioned the finest woods into regal inlaid furniture, baroque in its elaborateness.

Dressmaker details are a hallmark of New Orleans designer Gerrie Bremermann's far-from-basic window treatments. Here, intricate folds are worked into the curtain heading, while braid—flat trim first woven on the jacquard loom of the Napoléon era—creates a decisive edge. According to the late Sister Parish (1910–94), one of the most influential tastemakers of the twentieth century, "Curtains must always have an edge or an ending," a dictum adhered to here.

Facing Page: Holding most everything a breakfast room needs, a cupboard dating from the eighteenth century is clad in its original paint. Set against color-washed walls, it is topped with Chinese export china.

To suggest the look of a chic salon, fine French furniture is juxtaposed with equally impressive antiques. Black lacquered Régence chairs, swathed in an Old World Weavers' tiger stripe, flank the *lit de repros,* a daybed covered in a Scalamandré stripe. Napoléon was especially fond of stripes and used them lavishly in decorating both his state and private homes.

Facing Page: What was once a stable on a large New Orleans estate is today an inviting home. Reflecting a lifetime of avid collecting are a Napoléonic bench and an eighteenth-century *trumeau*—an overmantel with a mirror and painting. Exquisite miniature portraits painted on ivory, tortoiseshell, and silver date from the seventeenth, eighteenth, and nineteenth centuries.

A collection of nineteenth-century botanicals—purchased in one fell swoop—decorates an entrance-hall stairwell. Although no two frames are exactly alike, their similarities unite the space. The grouping is from The Gray Door, in Houston.

An entrance hall is not simply for welcoming guests or rushing through on the way to more important areas. Although not necessarily a room, it has the power to insure that important first impressions are positive and lasting. Stepping out of France is an exquisite mirror that hangs above a nineteenth-century *console*. With all things Italian also in fashion these days, faux-painted walls host eighteenth-century paintings—perhaps left by generations past.

As if also exhibiting proof of the court's unassailable wealth and authority, intricate tortoiseshell, brass, ivory, and mother-of-pearl were veneered into *marqueterie* patterns, exaggerating the beauty of each piece. Rich *ormolu*, or gilded bronze moldings and medallions, further defined elegance, enticing royals, nobles, and aristocrats eager to maintain their place in society to emulate the king's extravagances even when the largess was beyond their reach.

Fresh flowers are among the special touches that help create an intimate mood. The arrangement on the bedside table is by Jeffrey Lee and Rajan Patel, the creative forces behind Urban Flower in Stanley Korshak's chic Dallas floral shop.

Facing Page: For centuries, the bedroom was where high-level meetings took place, until Louis XV's renowned mistress, Madame de Pompadour—the arbiter of eighteenth-century taste—removed it from the list of public rooms. After that, it became worthy of being called a *boudoir*, which in French means a lady's private retreat.

One literally needed a title, however, to experience the majesty of the tall, ostentatious chairs with upholstered, haughty-looking backs and *stretchers* reinforcing the legs. Since only the self-indulgent king and his wife were allowed to sit in a *fauteuil*, or armchair, there were an abundance of *tabourets*, or lowly stools and benches—all robed in regal fabrics, including tapestry and embroidered silk.

Shimmering brocades lavishly threaded with gold, exquisite damasks, and splendid velvets garnished with handmade silk *passementerie*—fringes and tassels—took one's breath away. Famed Gobelin tapestries made in Paris and carpets on neutral grounds from Aubusson, Beauvais, and the merged Savonnerie and Gobelin factories presented a tantalizing glimpse of seventeenth-century decorative arts.

With all of Europe watching, ceilings and walls ablaze with *frescoes*—paintings on wet plaster with origins in fourteenth-century Italy—shamelessly begged to be noticed. Elaborately carved *boiserie*, gilded or spiced with gold leaf, replaced solid wood trim. And the dazzling Hall of

Voluminous silk taffeta, in one of Travers' iciest hues, is edged in a Houlès blue, marrying lightness and grandeur on a French rug dating from the 1920s. All are free of worries about *patrimoine*—the French law that strictly forbids unique or historically important works of art from leaving the country. Actually, in the last decades a number of countries, including Italy and Egypt, have banned the export of certain treasures.

On this side of the Atlantic, vintage crystal jars and perfume bottles elevate the daily ritual of putting on cosmetics. Hundreds of years ago, Madame de Pompadour ceremoniously encouraged courtiers to present themselves at an hour when she would be *à la toilette,* aware that she looked especially alluring at that time.

Mirrors, whose glass was made at Saint-Gobain and then silvered in Paris, gave a publicity boost to the king's insatiable appetite for excess. As a result, baroque furnishings became known on the Continent as Louis XIV, and the influence of the French replaced that of the Italians and Spanish. Over time, people on both sides of the Atlantic would name French furniture, in the design of the period, for the reigning king.

When Louis XIV died in 1715, his five-year-old great-grandson, whose parents and brother had passed away earlier, assumed the throne as Louis XV (1710–74) under the regency of his cousin (twice removed), Philippe II, the Duke of Orléans. When Philippe died in 1723, Cardinal de Fleury advised the young king from 1726 until 1743, at which time Louis XV governed alone until his own death in 1774.

The transitional period between the opulent baroque and the less formal rococo era of Louis XV became known as French Régence, or Regency. It should not be confused with the Regency era in England from 1811 to 1820, when the future George IV was named regent and furniture resembled the French Directoire period (1789–1804), with its Revolutionary motifs or the French Empire style of Napoléon and Josephine that followed (1800 to about 1850).

Offended by the unrestrained *ancien régime*, the endless ritualistic pageantry of Versailles, and even having the world at his feet, the *régent* moved the royal court to Paris, where courtiers lived in *hôtels particuliers*, or private residences, suited to a less pompous way of life without great fanfare. Perhaps inevitably, intimate *petit salons* ushered in an era of less cumbersome furniture with sweeping curves while rejecting the heavily carved baroque pieces of Louis XIV.

Shapely *cabriole* legs replaced straight ones on chairs, clocks, and case pieces—*armoires*, bookcases, and writing desks all designed as storage. With motifs inspired by the foliage of the region, delicate bouquets wrapped with ribbons and bows graced the upper sections of *armoires*.

Facing Page: A powder room tampers with perception by exuding passion for *trompe l'oeil*, a decorative technique rooted in ancient Rome. The term, however, is French. The sink—unearthed at the Marché aux Puces, the famed Paris flea market—was given a new life with fittings from Herbeau France; they are also available at Herbeau Creations of America, Naples, Florida.

A detail of a centerpiece that rivals anything created in France.

Facing Page: French style is reflected in a table set with considerable panache.

Preceding Overleaf: In this global art showcase is an antique Oushak area rug that hails from Turkey, plus an antique screen and late-eighteenth-century chandelier from France. Fortuny fabric, from the elegant Italian fabric company, embellishes the Louis XV daybed in a room pulled together by John Bobbitt of Dallas.

Rather than resting on their laurels, master cabinetmakers fashioned a low chest of drawers called a *commode*, which differed from the *bureau commode*, or large table with drawers that was crafted in the baroque period. Then, the *bombé commode*, with a puffed chest and plump sides, made a grand entrance. Startlingly beautiful wall paneling with softly curved corners also draped the French Régence era.

Furthermore, a fascination with the Far East, which had begun in 1670 when the Trianon de Porcelaine at Versailles was built for one of Louis XIV's mistresses, increased. When demand for all things Oriental—from silk screens and lacquered cabinets with gleaming varnished finishes to blue-and-white porcelain vases and embroidered hangings—outstripped supply, French craftsmen copied these richly decorated pieces, then added showy flourishes of their own to the ones that inspired them. The look brought together Far Eastern inspiration and Western craftsmanship, creating the foundation for the style known as *chinoiserie*, which is still fashionable today.

The Régence era pointed the way for the more beguiling rococo period (1730–60), when Louis XV and his official mistress *(maîtresse en titre)* Jeanne-Antoinette Poisson, or Madame de Pompadour, had great influence on the decorative arts. Though public reception rooms retained their sense of glamour and grandeur, family apartments were refashioned into less formal settings where strong colors were replaced with the pastels favored by Madame de Pompadour. With a new reserve embracing comfort, Louis XV sought inviting chairs, rather than stools, and fluid furniture arrangements conducive to talk.

As a result, the king's highly skilled *menuisier*, Jean-Baptiste Tilliard, sculpted a perfectly proportioned low, curved armchair with an exposed wood frame, far lighter and less regal-looking than any former chairs. On the seat rail of the *bergère*, he carved a basket of flowers. On its back, he shaped shells and *cartouches*, or fanciful scrolls, which communicated that this chair was not meant to stiffly line the wall but rather to be moved about for impromptu use.

As Parisian chairmakers began adopting Tilliard's designs, the frames of both caned and Louis XV *bergère* chairs were at times gilded or painted. Upholstered arms were moved back from the length of the seat so that *au courant* crinolines would not be crushed. When hooped skirts were no longer in vogue, they would again extend forward, but the soft, loose pillows still rested on fabric-covered platforms and curvaceous legs remained stretcher-free. Even centuries later, the rich damasks and velvets favored for upholstery would be seen as the height of chic.

Meanwhile, the *chaise longue* (in America spelled *chaise lounge*) emerged as a *tour de force* that Americans would come to embrace, followed by the *escritoire*—also called a secretary—a small desk with drawers and cubicles.

Painstaking carvings on wood pieces, some magnificent beyond description, were pulled from all aspects of nature, including shells, fish, waves, birds, vines, flowers, rocks, and serpents.

Above and Facing Page: The beauty of Paris has long inspired writers, musicians, and artists, including American architects. Behind this elegant, ivy-draped façade lies an attention to detail that exalts the splendors of France.

Some of the city's most sought-after *appartements* are tucked behind closed doors, such as these on Paris's Left Bank.

Facing Page: Heavy carved doors open onto the cobblestone courtyard of a *hôtel particular*, or private residence, off the grand Avenue des Champs Élysées, where, centuries ago, horse-drawn carriages invariably waited as enviable ladies gathered to pass the time with needlework or gossip, or sought other means of escaping from everyday constraints.

Also, designs were commonly rooted in farming motifs such as corn and wheat. Ribbons with streamers and hearts became popular, too.

By the second quarter of the eighteenth century, dwellings in Paris flashed brilliant crystal chandeliers and small, exquisitely carved marble mantels with large mirror panels, or painted overmantels called *trumeaux*. Wood floors were arranged in *marqueterie* patterns or in large Versailles-like *parquet* designs, and then warmed with alluring Aubusson or Savonnerie rugs.

Whereas the baroque style of Louis XIV exuded a passion for symmetry, firmly holding that any chair, room, or *château* divided vertically should be a precise mirrored-image half, the rococo style of Louis XV once again endorsed asymmetry, born in the Régence era.

Not everyone in France, however, was sold on grandeur, let alone gloss. Many people preferred the unpretentious beauty of pieces produced outside Paris that were redolent of woods in surrounding regions. If not quite astounding, *armoires* and *commodes* were sufficiently commanding—generously scaled, graceful, and easily identified by intricately carved decorative panels studded with exacting motifs. Eagles, flower baskets, and garden instruments, for instance, were the favored ornamentation in Lyon, Arles, and Nimes respectively, where furniture was sturdily crafted in walnut.

Others opted for the unassuming splendor of neoclassical style, replete with refined straight lines and striking proportions sans fussiness. In a conscientious retreat from obvious excess, Parisian *ébénistes* adopted motifs from ancient Greece and Italy's excavations of Herculaneum (1738) and nearby Pompeii (1748), adeptly creating furniture with more subtle details suiting Madame de Pompadour and her brother, the Marquis de Marigny, who were first struck by the fresh beauty of neoclassicism before the death of Louis XV.

During Louis XVI's reign (1774–92), he and his queen, Marie Antoinette, further defined neoclassical style with astonishing sureness. Although oak was valued for its hardness, the royal couple coveted case pieces crafted in mahogany, helping the wood to flourish in their distinctive decorative image. Also thanks to their unmistakable influence, ebony, which had fallen from favor after Louis XIV sat on the throne, returned to undisputed glory as demand mushroomed.

Partial to purple, the queen splashed private rooms in her favorite shades, washed wood pieces in dignified greenish-gray, and enveloped her Versailles boudoir with a *toile de Jouy*, while her husband decreed that the Oberkampf factory in the French town of Jouy-en-Josas, not far from the palace, be elevated to royal-supplier status.

In the place of extravagantly carved wall paneling, smartly understated *boiserie* modestly adorned with acanthus leaves and small rosettes ascended walls. No longer were ceilings covered with *frescoes*; instead, they remained plain, while doors, windows, and marble mantels outlined in thin moldings looked pleasingly elegant amid growing social unrest.

Differences aside, four French kings revolutionized decorating by crafting styles that would forever remain the personification of good taste. But by no means are the French alone in their appreciation. Transcending time zones and connecting cultures, seventeenth- and eighteenth-century furniture from Louis XIII to Louis XVI is highly sought the world over.

Facing Page: When botanicals climb the walls, a once-humble powder room takes on new vitality. Houston designer Dianne Josephs found both the antique prints and the artful borders in London shops, perhaps taking her cue from Empress Josephine Bonaparte, who was said to have taken extraordinary care over the smallest detail. Botanist that the Empress was, she had rare species of plants brought from all over the world to her gardens at Malmaison. The carved French *commode* has a new limestone top. Both mirror and *commode* are from Joyce Horn Antiques in Houston.

A light and airy garden room in the soft, watery colors favored by Madame de Pompadour sings with French style. The *pièce de résistance* is, of course, the antique opera seat from Lewis & Maese. (Opera diva Beverly Sills is said to own the matching one, though hers is tufted and upholstered in velvet.) But the room also boasts an antique Italian table, a Haines Bros. piano, and Bennison linen from England. A *papier-mâché* coffee table adds a note of whimsy. New York City decorative painter Hillary Harnischfeger embellished the walls and ceiling.

Facing Page: An old-fashioned screened porch runs the length of the house, offering a view of the outside world's seasonal splendor. Meanwhile, a savvy *café* table plants itself next to softly cooing doves—the answer to the frenzied pace of everyday life. Low-maintenance stone readily handles paw prints and breakfast spills, whereas lanterns add a posh touch.

Italian Panache

*O*pen my heart, and you will see

Graved inside of it, "Italy."

—*Robert Browning*

They call it bella figura. Like style, it is easy to recognize but cannot be simply explained. Loosely translated, the message, it seems, is that making a good impression is *everything*, which, naturally, is easier said than done. For doing so not only consumes enormous time and energy but also is comprised of endless possibilities darting in a blur—from the way one stands, speaks, walks, and dresses to one's manners and the manner in which one bedecks the home and entertains.

Indeed, *bella figura* means different things to different people, with varying interpretations clearly being shaped by interests and tastes when it comes to fashionable interior decorating and design. Some see it as rich colors, a savvy mix of fabrics from the finest mills, hand-painted antiques, and mellow old woods with warm patinas. For others, it is the luxury of comfort, interesting collections, and the veneer of elegance. And for still others, it is the improbable beauty found in distinctive details that flatter a room.

Say what you like: *bella figura* is not an easy thing to come by. Neither social cachet nor money offers any guarantee of making a positive impression. But,

Facing Page: In this stressful age, we long for our bathrooms to be calm retreats from the everyday world. And reminiscent, too, of respites at luxurious spas where leisure has been treasured among heated towel rails and gleaming European fittings that quiet the mind, soothe the senses, and befriend the spirit in satisfying doses. In short, we long to relax behind closed doors in marble-lined bathrooms with open showers and the subtle niceties of the one pictured here.

Preceding Overleaf: "Mangia bene, Vive bene," ("Eat well, Live well"), the saying that is an Italian icon, brings to mind thoughts of pasta—a traditional first course—followed by meat, game or fish. For eating well no longer means just pasta and *piazza* any more than living well requires suppressing one's taste and preferences. Here, glazed red cabinets keep clutter to a minimum. Easy-care stone sweeps countertops and floors. Further setting the kitchen apart is a gleaming stainless-steel stove, which is not reserved for a professional chef but does offer an endless variety of Italian dishes.

then, even in a demanding world we would never be content to let family name, net worth, or appearances define us—as that would be considered *gauche*.

It hardly matters, though. Despite cultural differences, the French and Italians alike have become our passports to good taste, the latter luring us with their passion for life, innate warmth, and reliable images. As if this were not enough, we look to the Italian people for unassuming ways—both obvious and subtle—of living, entertaining, and decorating.

Needless to say, our appetite for all that is Italian is not out of place. After all, few countries elicit awe quite like Italy. While its bureaucracy can be mystifying, its exceptional beauty is an ongoing feast for our admiring gaze, its tangled history, assimilated culture, and relaxed sophistication sources of endless fascination.

Seducing us are *case coloniche*—the typical Tuscan farmhouses steeped in countless charm; sun-bleached villas with easygoing elegance; and their extravagant, more celebrated cousins—sumptuous *palazzi* whose *au courant* proportions merit high praise. In the midst of such plenty are the landscapes that inspired Renaissance artists Leonardo da Vinci, Raphael, and Michelangelo, framed by vineyards, olive groves, and neat rows of cypress trees.

Fashionably appointed in the latest Italian taste, a master bedroom reads Milan—with its respectable bed by Lx Rossi, curtains and needlepoint shades that are works of art, upholstery from the Cameron Collection, and legendary Clarence House and Nobilis fabrics. Yet in 1240, it was Henry III of England who commissioned the first king-sized bed—an unforgettable *lit à colonne* (four-poster) with painted canopy and heavy curtains that not only protected him from drafts but also screened him from those passing through his chambers, as privacy was nonexistent.

For breakfast, many Italians enjoy something sweet: for example, a *corneto* (the Italian version of the French croissant) with jam inside and sugar on top, along with a *caffè latte*—an *espresso* with scalded milk and sugar added. So far the American coffeehouse Starbucks has no shops in Italy. However, it does have more than a thousand stores outside the United States.

Facing Page: A pleasing mix of Italian and French influences bridges the gap between two cultures. The tumbled marble on the backsplash is from Italy, while the cast-iron fireback behind the cooktop is French, circa 1830. In the seventeenth century, decorative metal liners called firebacks were placed at the backs of fireplaces to redirect heat into the room instead of up the flue. Firebacks also protected the masonry. While the basket holds pastas to suit every palate, the center island offers extra workspace for producing cuisine that transcends international borders.

In each of Italy's twenty-one regions resides unique character and charm, stemming from the customs, climate, and terrain. But it is centrally huddled Tuscany, Umbria, Marche, and Lazio, awash with old-world rhythms and a colorful air, that have given life to the style known as Italian Country, which has since proven irresistible. And no wonder. Despite exterior trappings or how intimate the enclosures, interiors resound with an unabashed reverence for beauty. Yet settings are distinctly Italian: expressive, airy, and, most importantly, inviting. Much like the country's undulating cities and towns, each has its own easy way of welcoming the steady flow of relatives and close friends central to life.

Never mind that Italy has a staggering number of congenial places to dine—some pricey, but also a wealth of reasonable *ristoranti* and even less-expensive small *trattorie*, or taverns, not to mention unpretentious *osterie*, or wine bars in busy neighborhoods that lend themselves to people-watching. Stopping by each other's homes is practically a daily ritual (which, in fact, may be why young men in Italy are all too often known as mama's boys), if not to share lingering meals, then for the sole purpose of doing nothing more than relaxing, thus preserving the tradition of *dolce far niente*, or sweet idleness, while sipping *espresso*.

Though tastes differ, unforgettable colors, sensuous textures, and fluid, natural fabrics—including revered Fortuny prints now printed on cotton only—mingle with customary Italian flair, gently jarring spaces that might otherwise appear too serious with a sense of delight.

While some young girls may take their inspiration from Kay Thompson's hyperactive Eloise, who orders from room service, rides elevators, and roams the halls of New York City's Plaza Hotel where she lives, Eloise would undoubtedly cast an approving eye on a more feminine yet less snobbish sort of place. An antique bench pays homage to the French, while sheers from Creation Baumann, Los Angeles, filter the light. Having all the makings of a family heirloom is the hand-painted Brazilian cabinet, a reproduction from the Roberta Schilling Collection in Miami.

Preceding Overleaf: Surrounding the trestle table made of aged wood are reproduction chairs with backs upholstered in hand-tooled leather. The uptown sofa, covered in Veronese hand-stamped velvet, is by Rob Jones. King Custom Draperies, of Houston, fabricated the pleated gray silk from Gretchen Bellinger as well as the Scalamandré silk panels. Beneath the Dutch landscape, dating from the nineteenth century, sits an eighteenth-century Italian server from Houston's Brian Stringer Antiques.

A kitchen sizzles with the allure of Italy when old-world styling meets forward-looking flair. As if trumpeting the country's penchant for innovative design, the beamed ceiling looks down on tile inlaid with individual pieces of hand-painted pottery, each different. The result is not only a visual treat but also a warmth most inviting.

Lunch in Italy is generally eaten at one o'clock; however, mealtime may stretch out for hours. Here, a distinctive octagonal space off the kitchen serves as the informal dining room. The backs of new Dennis & Leen chairs are upholstered in a Brunschwig & Fils fabric. Seats are covered in leather. Antique sconces circle the room, with each lauding a different motif relating to France.

At the side of a music room a daybed offers intimate seating, while a coffee table provides a place for drinks. The coffee table is an innovation of the last century.

In eighteenth-century France, powder rooms were intended for powdering one's wig. Nowadays a sculpted niche like this offers more than a place to primp; it captures endless admirers. With a contemporary air, the hand-carved stone vanity hides plumbing while layer upon layer of glaze gives rise to walls that look convincingly old. Decorative painting is by Jer Giles Artworks of Lancaster, Texas.

A panoply of styles and cultures mingle amiably, delivering the best of various worlds to an Italianate villa. But in the midst of such lofty grandeur, a limestone fireplace carved by Harold Clayton of Dallas unabashedly takes pride of place. This is not to say that anything could obscure the importance of the Oriental Soumak that anchors the room. The family room's understated elegance also stems from arrangements by Judy Blackman Floral Designs, Dallas.

Facing Page: In a triumph of ingenuity, a villa designed by Richard Drummond Davis reflects the classic architecture of Tuscany. Soaring stone stairs, some with fossil traces, imbue the home with old-world sophistication, yet it is stocked with more amenities than most five-star hotels.

Admittedly, Americans have a passion for beautiful handmade lamps. A Fortuny-like hand-painted silk chandelier accessorized with beads hangs from the ceiling above the bed.

Left. An Italianate painted bed—the Friuli from Patina—along with the firm's Veneto *bombé* chest elevate off-hand glamour, while a rare Persian Mahal Sultanabad antique area rug anchors the room. Meters of fabrics and *passementerie,* plus *objets d'art* culled from abroad, further the classic European country ambience.

The master bedroom is home to this late-eighteenth-century Louis XV settee, which is also known as a *canapé* in France—or more specifically still as an *ottomane*, given that it is basket-shaped with an enclosed back that arcs gracefully forward. It was purchased at Kay O'Toole, Houston, then reupholstered in a Veronese hand-printed velvet.

In Italian bathrooms, where the palette rarely strays from the neutrals, soft white towels, bath oils, and scented sea salts with stress-relieving properties are not enough to bathe one in luxury. Natural light ranks near the top of priority lists. Jostling for space beside the Peter Fasano wallcovering are mosaics in the style of the Roman Empire from Walker Zanger. The curtain is constructed with Nancy Corzine fabric. Houston designer Marilyn Phillips happened upon the terra-cotta urn dating to the nineteenth century at Marchè de la Porte de Vanves, in Paris.

France and Italy mingle adeptly in a powder room brimming with antiques. The étagère, mirror, and pair of porcelain hand-painted tiles are all French, dating from the nineteenth century. From the same era is an unseen Italian chandelier.

Facing Page: Pride of place goes to ten-foot-tall oils on canvas—one unseen—that in the nineteenth century hung in a Paris bistro. Which is not to say the collection of vintage mercury glass, or silver glass, as some experts say the *objets d'art* adorning the dining table should be known, is not deserving of attention. Once also called "poor man's silver," vases such as these French flea-market finds are nowadays boldly sought. At night, shimmering candlelight adds to the gathering's glow.

Somehow, the sturdy silhouettes of finely crafted *commodes*, tables, and chairs with a former life manage to speak for themselves, without any one piece being too forward. Chandeliers worthy of the country's artisans flicker in eye-catching mirrors hung opposite one another, giving even small quarters more presence—though size, Italians argue, has nothing to do with style.

Since there is an aversion to heavy window treatments, tiebacks are shunned in favor of free-hanging curtains with minimum fuss. Memorably patterned stone floors meanwhile bask in one another's reflected glow, rarely spoiled by rugs.

Faithful to their heritage, antique tapestries meander through unpretentious villa halls, accompanied by cherished centuries-old paintings, some in need of cleaning. In truth, there is little doubt these days that most families live amid furnishings collected over several lifetimes, thoughtfully handed down generation after generation by caring ancestors—as if confirming once and for all what Americans have known all along: being the favorite has its privileges.

While next of kin may vie for a desk piped in history or covet a mosaic-topped table and a *commode* with *marqueterie* finer than another, in reality, living spaces are generally sparsely furnished and, almost without exception, shy of pretension. Quite simply, in Italy affectation has no place. And neither does clutter that might deter guests from moving about freely during, say, a pre-opera buffet.

True to tradition, comfort abounds—meaning that artistic merit does not take precedence over indulging family or pampering friends. Beside a chair, there is always a table big enough for a glass of wine and small plate of cheese with sliced salami and olives; there are pillows to relax against; soft, clinging shawls to gather for added warmth; and table and floor lamps placed just so for ending the day with *La Repubblica* or

Facing Page: Once upon a time, children's rooms had to look juvenile. But what a difference a few decades make. Today, schoolgirls are much more sophisticated. To be forever cherished is the vintage writing table—freshly painted in Italy—culled from Brian Stringer Antiques, Houston, plus a custom-colored four-poster bed from Jane Keltner Designs in Memphis. French prints dating from the nineteenth century were discovered in the Paris flea market Marchè Serpette. Meters of "Les Jardinanglais" from Marvic Textiles lead the way to stylish bedcovers. Parchment wallcovering is by Zoffany.

In a dining room with a degree of formality, there is a sense of comforting richness. While stainless silver becomes duller with use, sterling ages gracefully, as long as it is used rather than kept in a cloth-lined drawer. Although European flatware is larger than that produced in America, American sterling has a higher silver-to-copper ratio, as if polishing its image by honoring the universally accepted .925 standard established in the fourteenth century. But because Continental pieces are bigger, the weight of silver grams is generally higher. Just as importantly, though, Italian and French flatware feels as luxuriant as it looks, and that is what makes it so appealing.

A chorus of chairs in concert with rich woods and antiques culled from American sources are key to a music room's harmony.

Houston designers Clair and Cecilia Tally transported their chic style to a classic villa, creating a smartly dressed breakfast room that makes each new day ever more special.

With elegant ease rather than the haughty look of Parisian domains, a family room evokes a feeling of casual grandeur that encourages guests to linger.

A detail of the master bed. The hand-painted Italian chest offers extra storage. The Aubusson pillows are antique. The French sunburst, circa 1880, is another flea-market find.

Preceding Overleaf: In a master bedroom, Dallas designer Margaret Chambers pairs seductive chocolate with tones of cream and taupe that melt to create understated bark. Flannel interlining adds weight to the bed hangings and curtains, giving them an appearance that is unmistakably grand.

On a wall in the master bedroom stands a late-nineteenth-century hand-carved French bookcase laden with treasures that blur the boundaries between Italy and France. From Italy come hand-painted prints and antique hand-tooled leather boxes, while the altarsticks traveled from France and were later made into lamps.

Abroad, street markets brim with vegetables, fruits, and flowers bound for European homes. Rivaling the charm of rural Italy, hand-painted tile frames a kitchen window here in the States. The admirable field tile is from Walker Zanger showrooms, nationwide.

Facing Page: A sophisticated mix of Italian tableware from Stanley Korshak, Dallas, radiates Mediterranean splendor, while centuries-old Italian prints and an antique platter paint this dining room with further importance. The stone urn was stumbled upon in France. The reproduction table and chairs are worthy of the setting.

another of Italy's well-known daily papers. (Low lights are for entertaining only.) There is even a chair next to the bathtub for stacking towels, placing a robe, or relaxing upon while the tub fills.

Although the commonplace has never received the universal admiration of more important Italian pieces, the deft layering of the conventional with the glamourous makes stylish living look effortless, which is no small feat.

As it is, stately andirons, antique altarsticks, priceless clocks, and libraries of leather-bound books project an air of authority, while firescreens, planters, close-ups of family and friends, and bountiful bouquets, smartly arranged, plump settings with backdrops for handling the cares, concerns, and aspirations of everyday life.

Without fail, and without the princely prices of Le Sirenuse and other luxury hotels on the thirty-mile stretch of Amalfi Coast, impeccably pressed linens stretch across beds, hinting of femininity. Down-filled bolsters sprawl beneath soft down pillows as feather beds snuggle against mattresses. Modest box springs appear tightly wrapped in blanket covers, shielded from prying eyes.

Given that Italians balk at like furnishings lacking character, most cannot imagine awakening in a bed flanked by identical night tables covered with similar lamps, resting near a matching dresser or chests of drawers. Not that the younger generation, any less than their parents, does not consider *nonna's armoire* a wardrobe necessity. It does. But filling empty rooms with shiny new suites without any mystique, rather than mismatched antique pieces, is not something they understand.

Facing Page: A family room isn't complete without a cushy sofa, comfy pillows, and good-looking chairs. Add some imposing antiques, an unforgettable sunflower bouquet, and a collection of design books, and you have the makings of the perfect setting for lingering over coffee or talking about ambitions.

To their way of thinking, it is unpardonable to live in a house full of rootless pieces with no ties to the past or any sentiment attached. Furnishings must be as meaningful as they are decorative, with the secrets and bruises of history opening a window into the Italian way of life.

In a bow to Italian life, Florentino chairs surround a dining table from Genoa while the floor is paved in antique brick. The *console* was found in northern France—so close to the Italian border it is hard to pinpoint its origin. Upon it sit charming, hard-working *crèche* figures called *santos*, meaning little saints, rooted in sixteenth-century Italy when public displays of faith were banned. The ones seen here actually are from Spain and Portugal, dating from the eighteenth and nineteenth centuries. The painting is by Fleur Cowles, publisher of the fabled *Flair* magazine.

Left: A former servants' kitchen gave way to an inviting breakfast room reminiscent of the nineteenth century. Charm comes from the color-washed terra-cotta walls, a painted *armoire* happened upon in Tuscany, and the adored dog. Antique plates are Limoge, from the French city known for its porcelain.

Plying a reading room with worldly style are graceful, beautifully proportioned pieces. The painted cabinet serves as a dramatic focal point, providing storage for everything from engraved correspondence cards to classical compact discs.

Facing Page: A magnificent seventeenth-century Portuguese headboard shrouded in mystery offers a priceless glimpse of the past. Meanwhile, the Louis XVI settee shows off its fluted legs, plus a sexy silhouette. Dusted-off family heirlooms set the mood. Ancient Romans used both gilt and gold to define social position and wealth.

Points of View

One of the most attractive things about flowers is their beautiful reserve.

—*Henry David Thoreau*

By now everyone knows that Venice is sinking three-quarters of an inch every year. Not only that, but also that restoring a villa in Italy is far from a walk in the park, since municipalities each have their own building commissions and mysterious rules dedicated to preserving local architecture.

The classic Italian garden is as carefully planned as rooms inside the Italianate villa, reflecting centuries-old Roman thinking that the surroundings of a dwelling are as significant as the design of the residence itself. Indeed, few people anywhere are as interested in the harmonious union of space and shape as those living in Italy. It's a small wonder that even the most modest house generally has its garden—and that those gardens have inspired imitators all over the world.

Grounded in order and symmetry, labyrinthine patterns of ilex, laurel, and cypress trees frame shimmering pools and showering fountains set between gravel paths, while mazes of common box hedges and yews sculpted into spheres, cones, globes, and pyramids divide spaces into gracious outdoor rooms—arbors, pergolas, and grottoes—draped in wisteria. Foliage is in keeping with the scale of sites while sharing property rights with age-worn mythological statuary too beautiful to ignore.

Preceding Overleaf: With their regal presence and overpowering beauty, wrought-iron gates hint at the graciousness within a private world reflecting the glory of France.

A secluded estate takes its cue from Marie Antoinette, whose summer getaway, Le Hameau, was draped in lacy swathes of heavily scented wisteria.

Italy was also once enamored with daffodils, tulips, and paper whites. However, try as one might, bulbs often failed to thrive on a peninsula that burns in intense sunlight most of the year. After years of proving too costly and difficult to maintain, other perennials slowly vanished from classic Italian gardens, too. Instead landscapers planted strong, compelling lines of less-thirsty greenery within balustrades of stone and stucco, embraced inviting waters, and focused their creative energies on constructing imposing walls using stones quarried nearby.

In 1563, Florentine queen Catherine de Médici brought to France a penchant for thoughtfully planned, well-groomed gardens when she purchased property on the banks of the Seine from the Tuileries for an Italian-style park in the heart of Paris. But it was the Sun King, Louis XIV, and his landscape designer, André Le Nôtre, who fashioned a carpet of even more astonishing beauty—the magnificent gardens of Versailles on the outskirts of the city. With the palace meticulously centered on the site and, behind it, not a square meter of land ignored, the sweeping views gave an impression of limitless grandeur.

Born in Paris in 1613, André Le Nôtre was the son and grandson of royal gardeners. Faithful to family tradition, he succeeded his father, Jean Le Nôtre, at the Jardin des Tuileries when the latter became head gardener to Louis XIII—just as Jean Le Nôtre had followed in his own father's footsteps at the Tuileries when he was summoned in 1592 to serve as landscaper to Queen Marie de Médici.

André Le Nôtre was recognized as a gifted engineer as well as a passionate gardener. With a fresh way of seeing the world, in 1637 he set about revamping Tuileries—originally a rubbish dump with clay soil used for making tiles *(tuiles)*; hence its name. To begin with, he raised terraces, created a central lane vista, and carved out pools. Gaining momentum, he lined the grounds with trees and hedges and embellished the land with fountains, pavilions, and statuary, shaping a formal, geometric extension of the Louvre, which would soon come to be considered

Facing Page: Seducing guests in the carefree Mediterranean mood is a spacious loggia that looks out on a pool and is designed for alfresco dining. Dramatic stucco arches supported by Tuscan-style columns add rhythm to the façade while framing the sitting area decked in weather-resistant fabrics.

the world's greatest art museum. Years later, in 1667, he would craft the regal Avenue des Champs-Élysées, giving the wide boulevard even more presence by lacing it with parallel rows of chestnut trees and planting flower gardens.

Expressing his artistic visions, Le Nôtre worked tirelessly from 1656 to 1661 producing an extraordinary masterpiece for Nicolas Fouquet, Louis XIV's minister of finances. After redirecting one of two rivers traversing unspoiled terrain at Vaux-le-Vicomte—in the town of Seine-et-Marne, south of Paris—Le Nôtre carefully arranged a hierarchy of small spaces spawned from a central axis that swept into distant views. Flower-banked reflecting pools, basins, and waterfalls, as well as 1,200 fountains, offered further proof of his distinctive ideas and of his creative hand.

With obvious pride, Fouquet hosted a glittering fête on the evening of August 17, 1661, celebrating completion of the three-kilometer (about 1.5-mile) horticultural extravaganza. Against this backdrop of splendor and beauty, six thousand guests—including the king and his entire royal court—dined, danced, and were entertained by bursts of fireworks.

The night might have been successful had it not sparked grudging admiration and jealousy. Outside France, those familiar with the project praised the accomplishment. But while royals on the Continent sought Le Nôtre's services, a provoked king seethed over everything—from being

A winding avenue leads to showering water shaded by trees.

Preceding Overleaf: With a grandeur reflecting its worldly occupants, a sumptuous *château* stands neither cracked nor crumbled by time. But then, it is not the typical dwelling that one sees outside a hundred French towns on the standard road trip from Paris to the Rivera. Rather, it is the *ne plus ultra* of *châteaux*—a master's house, or *maison de maitre*, firmly planted on American soil.

Facing Page: A stately country house with grand proportions and ivy-covered stone arches is typical of houses of European nobility. Come summer, relaxed alfresco dinners will be served on the terrace.

Below: A closed door in a stone wall signals the garden is still sleeping. But it will soon open to a parade of springtime flowers. Among the daffodils, crocuses, and tulips, antique fountains and statuary—from both France and Italy—share star billing, while urns weathered by time vie for rights to the terrace.

upstaged by breathtaking gardens to Fouquet's glaringly obvious good taste to his failure to follow the period's rigidly hierarchical standards of behavior.

It was universally understood that subjects were expected to obey the strict class rules of the time, and, in the king's mind, Nicolas Fouquet's bravura was unseemly. As a result, little more than three weeks after those gathered had applauded in delight—on September 5, the king's twenty-third birthday—he imprisoned the minister of finances for life. To recover his lost glory, Louis XIV also sent for the artist responsible for the landscaping at Vaux-le-Vicomte, challenging him to exceed all prior triumphs at Versailles.

And it appears that Le Nôtre did. For no one would argue that he created a predilection for French gardens when most of the world was still enamored by Italian ones.

When André Le Nôtre died in 1700, France mourned the loss of the most famous landscape architect of the seventeenth century. Yet his unprecedented influence is still strongly felt as people from far-flung corners of the globe continue taking their cues from his awe-inspiring designs, including the sprawling Palace at Versailles, landscaped more than three centuries ago.

In America, emerald gardens of French and Italian descent adhere strictly to general plans that are equally mindful of the same key elements: logic, order, discipline, and beauty. Whether the land is rolling or flat, gravel paths separate well-defined patterns of squares and rectangles. Plantings sectioned into smaller beds captivatingly boast mirror images. Meanwhile, statuary, fountains, and urns spilling over with foliage add majestic dimensions to estates not necessarily as posh or formal as many of those abroad.

Appropriately, then, we salute the exhilarating style of the French and Italian people that compels interpretation half a world away. Yet we insist on scripting our own spaces, trusting our own artistry, and expressing without apology our own points of view. That André Le Nôtre disliked flowers barely matters. Blossoms brighten American spirits as we look to the future while looking back.

Above: Water streams gently from a fountain once warmed by the Provençal sun.

Below: Far from their original home in Provence rest signed olive oil jars dating from the eighteenth century. More bulbous jars were made in the nineteenth century.

In shade cast by tall trees, heirloom iron furniture offers an ideal spot for gathering or quietly reading a book. Combining country comfort with European grandeur is an enduring Tuscan legacy left behind by American architect David Adler (1882–1949). Built in 1927 in Colorado Springs, Colorado, the house boasts the prevalent terra-cotta hue that splashes Italy.

Facing Page: Serving as an outdoor gathering spot for alfresco luncheons, as well as a meeting point between the landscape and the David Adler house, is an arbor that frames a postcard-perfect view. Vintage Spanish chairs surround the Tuscan table.

Page 184: A garden room that is a study of interesting textures and shapes has its moment in the sun. Travers cotton—woven with a chenille stripe—hangs in the windows. Matching Charles Pollack settees sport Old World Weavers fern-covered linen, while the hand-painted chest further links indoors and out. Both the chest and the coffee table are by Patina, the world's leading maker of Venetian-inspired furnishings this side of the eighteenth century. The urn is an antique.

Page 185: Bocce (pronounced BOHT-cheh) is the national game of Italy, enjoyed by nobility and peasants alike. The Romans learned the game from the Greeks, then introduced it throughout the empire. Much like lawn bowling, it is generally played on a long, narrow dirt court. George Washington built a bocce ball court at Mount Vernon in the last quarter of the eighteenth century.

Magnifique in America

$\mathscr{T}$hought is the seed

of action.

—*Ralph Waldo Emerson*

ANTIQUE FURNISHINGS AND ACCESSORIES

America Antiques and Design
Five South Main Street
Lambertville, NJ 08530
Telephone: 609.397.6966
www.americadesigns.com

Agostino Antiques Ltd.
808 Broadway at 11th Street
New York, NY 10003
Telephone: 212.533.3355

Brian Stringer Antiques
2031 West Alabama Street
Houston, TX 77006
Telephone: 713.526.7380

Burden & Izell, Ltd.
180 Duane Street
New York, NY 10013
Telephone: 212.941.8247

Carl Moore Antiques
1610 Bissonnet Street
Houston, TX 77005
Telephone: 713.524.2502

Challiss House
463 Jackson Street
San Francisco, CA 94111
Telephone: 415.397.6999

Charles Gaylord Antiques
2151 Powell Street
San Francisco, CA 94133
Telephone: 415.392.6085

Country French Interiors
1428 Slocum Street
Dallas, TX 75207
Telephone: 214.747.4700

Dixon & Dixon
237 Royal Street
New Orleans, LA 70130
Telephone: 800.848.5148

Duane
176 Duane Street
New York, NY 10013
Telephone: 212.625.8066

Ed Hardy San Francisco, Inc.
188 Henry Adams Street
San Francisco, CA 94103
Telephone: 415.626.6300
www.edhardysf.com

Fireside Antiques
14007 Perkins Road
Baton Rouge, LA 70810
Telephone: 225.752.9565
www.firesideantiques.com

The French Attic
The Stalls
116 Bennett Street
Atlanta, GA 30309
Telephone: 404.352.4430

The Gables
711 Miami Circle
Atlanta, GA 30324
Telephone: 800.753.3342
www.thegablesantiques.com

Galerie de France
184–186 Duane Street
New York, NY 10013
Telephone: 212.965.0969

Gore Dean Antiques
2828 Pennsylvania Avenue
Washington, DC 20007
Telephone: 202.625.1776

The Gray Door
1809 West Gray Street
Houston, TX 77019
Telephone: 713.521.9085

Hideaway House
143 North Robertson Boulevard
Los Angeles, CA 90048
Telephone: 310.276.4319

Inessa Stewart Antiques
8630 Perkins Road
Baton Rouge, LA 70810
Telephone: 225.769.9363

Inessa Stewart Antiques
5201 West Lovers Lane
Dallas, TX 75209
Telephone: 214.366.2660

J. H. Antiques
174 Duane Street
New York, NY 10013
Telephone: 212.965.1443

Jacqueline Adams
2300 Peachtree Road NW,
  Suite B 110
Atlanta, GA 30309
Telephone: 404.355.8123

Jane J. Marsden Antiques
2300 Peachtree Road NW
Atlanta, GA 30309
Telephone: 404.355.1288
www.marsdenantiques.com

Jane Moore Interiors
2922 Virginia Street
Houston, TX 77098
Telephone: 713.526.6113

John Rosselli & Associates, Ltd.
523 East 73rd Street
New York, NY 10021
Telephone: 212.772.2137

John Rosselli & Associates, Ltd.
255 East 72nd Street
New York, NY 100121
Telephone: 212.737.2252

Joseph Minton Antiques
1410 Slocum Street
Dallas, TX 75207
Telephone: 214.744.3111
www.mintonantiques.com

Joyce Horn Antiques
1008 Wirt Road
Houston, TX 77055
Telephone: 713.688.0507

Junque
2303 A Dunlavy Street
Houston, TX 77006
Telephone: 713.529.2177

Le Louvre
1313 Slocum Street
Dallas, TX 75207
Telephone: 214.752.2605

Legacy Antiques
1406 Slocum Street
Dallas, TX 75207
Telephone: 214.748.4606

The Lotus Collection
445 Jackson Street
San Francisco, CA 94111
Telephone: 415.398.8115

Made In France
2912 Ferndale Place
Houston, TX 77098
Telephone: 713.529.7949

Mariette Himes Gomez
506 East 74th Street
New York, NY 10021
Telephone: 212.288.6856

Marston Luce
1651 Wisconsin Avenue NW
Washington, DC 20007
Telephone: 202.775.9460

The Mews
1708 Market Center Blvd.
Dallas, TX 75207
Telephone: 214.748.9070

Newell Art Galleries, Inc.
425 East 53rd Street
New York, NY 10022
Telephone: 212.758.1970
www.newell.com

Niall Smith
306 East 61st Street
New York, NY 10021
Telephone: 212.750.3985

Nick Brock Antiques
2909 North Henderson St.
Dallas, TX 75206
Telephone: 214.828.0624

Orion Antique Importers
1435 Slocum Street
Dallas, TX 75207
Telephone: 214.748.1177

Parc Monceau, Ltd.
45 D Bennett Street NW
Atlanta, GA 30309
Telephone: 404.355.3766

Patina Atelier Antiques
3364 Sacramento Street
San Francisco, CA 94118
Telephone: 415.409.2299

Sidney Lerer
420 Richmond Avenue
Pt. Pleasant Beach, NJ 08741
Telephone: 732.899.8949

South of Market
345 Peachtree Hills Avenue
Atlanta, GA 30305
Telephone: 404.995.9399

The Whimsey Shoppe Slocum
1444 Oak Lawn
Dallas, TX 75207
Telephone: 214.745.1800

Therien & So.
716 N. La Cienega Boulevard
Los Angeles, CA 90069
Telephone: 310.657.4615

Uncommon Market, Inc.
2701 Fairmount
Dallas, TX 75201
Telephone: 214.871.2775

Watkins, Schatte, Culver,
   Gardner
2308 Bissonnet Street
Houston, TX 77005
Telephone: 713.529.0597

BATH FITTINGS

Czech & Speake
350 11th Street
Hoboken, NJ 07030
Telephone: 800.632.4165
www.homeportfolio.com

Kallista, Inc.
2446 Verna Court
San Leandro, CA 94577
Telephone: 888.4.Kallista
www.kallistainc.com

St. Thomas Creations, Inc.
1022 West 24th Street, #125
National City, CA 91950
Telephone: 619.474.9490
www.stthomascreations.com

Sherle Wagner, International
60 East 57th Street
New York, NY 10022
Telephone: 212.758.3300
www.sherlewagner.com

Waterworks
60 Backus Avenue
Danbury, CT 06810
Telephone: 800.899.6757
www.waterworks.com

FABRICS AND WALLCOVERINGS

Anna French
Classic Revivals
One Design Center Place,
   Suite 534
Boston, MA 02210
Telephone: 617.574.9030

Bennison Fabrics
76 Greene Street
New York, NY 10012
Telephone: 212.941.1212

Bergamo Fabrics
7 West 22nd Street, 2nd Floor
New York, NY 10011
Telephone: 212.462.1010
www.bergamofabrics.com

Brunschwig & Fils, Inc.
75 Virginia Road
North White Plains, NY 10603
Telephone: 914.684.5800
www.brunschwig.com

Carlton V
D & D Building
979 Third Avenue, 15th Floor
New York, NY 10022
Telephone: 212.355.4525

Christopher Norman Inc
41 W. 25th Street, 10th Floor
New York, NY 10010
Telephone: 212.647.0303
www.christophernorman.com

Clarence House
211 East 58th Street
New York, NY 10022
Telephone: 212.752.2890
www.clarencehouse.com

Coraggio Textiles
1750 132nd Avenue NE
Bellevue, WA 98005
Telephone: 425.462.0035
www.coraggio.com

Cowtan & Tout
111 Eighth Avenue, Suite 930
New York, NY 10011
Telephone: 212.647.6900

Elizabeth Dow, Ltd.
155 Sixth Avenue, 4th Floor
New York, NY 10013
Telephone: 212.219.8822

Fortuny, Inc.
D & D Building
979 Third Avenue, 16th Floor
New York, NY 10022
Telephone: 212.753.7153
www.fortunyonline.com

Haas
50 Dey Street, Building One
Jersey City, NJ 07306
Telephone: 201.792.5959

Hinson & Company
2735 Jackson Avenue
Long Island City, NY 11101
Telephone: 718.482.1100

J. Robert Scott
500 North Oak Street
Inglewood, CA 90302
Telephone: 310.680.4300
www.jrobertscott.com

Jane Shelton
205 Catchings Avenue
Indianola, MS 38751
Telephone: 800.530.7259
www.janeshelton.com

Jim Thompson
1694 Chantilly Drive
Atlanta, GA 30324
Telephone: 800.262.0336
www.jimthompson.com/
   branch.html

Lee Jofa
225 Central Avenue South
Bethpage, NY 11714
Telephone: 888.LeeJofa
www.leejofa.com

Manuel Canovas
111 Eighth Avenue, Suite 930
New York, NY 10011
Telephone: 212.647.6900

Marvic Textiles
30–10 41st Avenue, 2nd Floor
Long Island City, NY 11101
Telephone: 718.472.9715

Nancy Corzine
256 West Ivy Avenue
Inglewood, CA 90302
Telephone: 310.672.6775

Nobilis
57-A Industrial Road
Berkeley Heights, NJ 07922
Telephone: 800.464.6670
www.nobilis.fr

Old World Weavers
D & D Building
979 Third Avenue
New York, NY 10022
Telephone: 212.355.7186

Osborne & Little
90 Commerce Road
Stamford, CT 06902
Telephone: 203.359.1500
www.osborneandlittle.com

Payne Fabrics
1000 Fountain Parkway
Grand Prairie, TX 75050
Telephone: 800.527.2517
www.westgatefabrics.com

Percheron
G6 Chelsea Harbour Design
   Centre
London SW 10 OXE
Telephone: 011.44.020.7349.
   1590

Peter Fasano, Ltd.
964 South Main Street
Great Barrington, MA 01230
Telephone: 413.528.6872

Pierre Frey, Inc.
12 East 33rd Street
New York, NY 10016
Telephone: 212.213.3099

Pollack & Associates
150 Varick Street
New York, NY 10013
Telephone: 212.627.7766

Prima Seta Silks/Jagtar & Co.
3073 N. California Street
Burbank, CA 91505
Telephone: 818.729.9333

Quadrille
50 Dey Street, Building One
Jersey City, NJ 07306
Telephone: 201.792.5959

Robert Allen
55 Cabot Boulevard
Mansfield, MA 02048
Telephone: 800.240.8189

Rogers & Goffigon
41 Chestnut Street
Greenwich, CT 06830
Telephone: 203.532.8068

Rose Cumming
Fine Arts Building
232 E. 59th Street, 5th Floor
New York, NY 10022
Telephone: 212.758.0844

Scalamandrè
300 Trade Zone Drive
Ronkonkoma, NY 11779
Telephone: 631.467.8800
www.scalamandre.com

Schumacher Company
79 Madison Ave., 14th Floor
New York, NY 10016
Telephone: 212.213.7900
www.fschumacher.com

Silk Trading Co.
360 S. La Brea Avenue
Los Angeles, CA 90036
Telephone: 323.954.9280
www.silktrading.com

Travers
504 East 74th Street
New York, NY 10021
Telephone: 212.772.2778
www.traversinc.com

FURNITURE

Cameron Collection
150 Dallas Design Center
1025 North Stemmons Fwy.
Dallas, TX 75207
Telephone: 214.744.1544

Charles P. Rogers
55 West 17th Street
New York, NY 10011
Telephone: 212.675.4400
www.charlesprogers.com

Dennis & Leen
8734 Melrose Avenue
Los Angeles, CA 90069
Telephone: 310.652.0855

The Farmhouse Collection
807 Russet Street
Twin Falls, ID 83301
Telephone: 208.736.8700

Gregorius/Pineo
653 N. La Cienga Boulevard
Los Angeles, CA 90069
Telephone: 310.659.0588

Hamilton, Inc.
8417 Melrose Place
Los Angeles, CA 90069
Telephone: 323.655.9193

Jane Keltner
94 Cumberland Boulevard
Memphis, TN 38112
Telephone: 800.487.8033
www.janekeltner.com

Niermann Weeks
Fine Arts Building
232 East 59th Street, 1st Floor
New York, NY 10022
Telephone: 212.319.7979
www.niermannweeks.com

Old Timber Table Company
908 Dragon Street
Dallas, TX 75207
Telephone: 214.761.1882

Patina, Inc.
351 Peachtree Hills Ave. NE
Atlanta, GA 30304
Telephone: 800.635.4365
www.patinainc.com

Randolph & Hein, Inc.
2222 Palou Street
San Francisco, CA 94124
Telephone: 415.864.3371

Rose Tarlow/Melrose House
8454 Melrose Place
Los Angeles, CA 90069
Telephone: 323.653.2122

Shannon & Jeal
722 Steiner Street
San Francisco, CA 94117
Telephone: 415.563.2727

Smith & Watson
200 Lexington Avenue,
 Suite 801
New York, NY 10016
Telephone: 212.686.6444

Summer Hill, Ltd
2682 Middlefield Road
Redwood City, CA 94063
Telephone: 650.363.2600
www.summerhill.com

Michael Taylor Designs
1500 Seventeenth Street
San Francisco, CA 94107
Telephone: 415.558.9940

IRON WORK

Brun Metal Crafts, Inc.
2791 Industrial Lane
Bloomfield, CO 80020
Telephone: 303.466.2513

Ironies
2222 Fifth Street
Berkeley, CA 94710
Telephone: 510.644.2100

Murray's Iron Work
5915 Blackwelder Street
Culver City, CA 90232
Telephone: 866.649.4766

Potter Art Metal
4500 North Central
 Expressway
Dallas, TX 75206
Telephone: 214.821.1419
www.potterartmetal.com

STONE AND TILE

Ann Sacks Tile & Stone
8120 NE 33rd Drive
Portland, OR 97211
Telephone: 800.969.5217
www.annsacks.com

Country Floors
15 East 16th Street
New York, NY 10003
Telephone: 212.627.8300
www.countryfloors.com

Paris Ceramics
151 Greenwich Avenue
Greenwich, CT 06830
Telephone: 888.845.3487
www.parisceramics.com

Walker Zanger
13190 Telfair Avenue
Sylmar, CA 91342
Telephone: 877.611.0199
www.walkerzanger.com

Photographic Credits

Designers

Roberto Agnolini: 166–167, 168, 169, 182, 183.

John Bobbitt: Title page, 112, 113, 115, 116–117, 118, 119, 120, 121, 170–171.

Gerrie Bremermann: 102, 104, 105, 106, 107, 181.

Margaret Chambers: Front cover, 158–159, 160, 161, 162, 163, 164.

Donald Coan: 94–95, 96, 98–99, 100–101, 176-177, 178, 179.

Sherry Hayslip: 144, 145.

Jerry Jeanmard: 186–187, 188.

Dianne Josephs: 108, 109, 125, 126, 127.

John Kidd: Opposite copyright, 16–17, 18, 66, 67, 68, 69, 72–73, 74, 76, 77, 92, 130, 132–133, 134, 135, 136–137, 138–139.

Janie Petkus: 80, 81.

Betty Lou Phillips: 86–87, 122, 123.

Christina Phillips: 15, 61, 62, 63, 75, 78, 79, 184.

Marilyn Phillips: 15, 61, 62, 63, 75, 78, 79, 128–129, 146–147, 148, 149, 150, 151, 153, 184.

Lynn Sears: 6–7, 26, 27, 56–57, 64, 65, 140, 141, 142, 143, 174.

Tony Stavish: 8–9, 11, 82–83.

Clair Talley: 154, 155, 156, 157, 172.

Robert H. Theriot: 40, 41, 42, 43, 48, 49, 55, 58, 60.

Richard Trimble: 28, 30–31, 32–33, 34, 35, 84–85, 103.

Rebecca Turner Wiggins: 50, 51.

Deborah Walker: 12–13, 20, 21, 22, 23, 24, 25, 36–37, 38, 39, 44–45, 46–47, 52, 53, 54, 70, 71, 88–89, 90, 91, 110, 111.

Architects

Richard Drummond Davis: 144.

Patrick Lynch Ford: 154, 156, 172.

Robbie Fusch: 28, 30–31, 32–33, 34.

Cole Smith: Front cover, 40, 41, 42, 43, 49, 55.

Weldon Turner: 6–7, 26, 56–57.

Elby S. Martin: 176–177, 180.

Photographers

Craig Dugan for Hedrich Blessing Photographers: 80.

Nancy Edwards: 173.

Janet Lenzen: Opposite copyright, 16–17, 18, 66, 67, 68, 69, 72–73, 74, 76, 77, 92, 108, 109, 125, 126, 127, 128–129, 130, 132–133, 134, 135, 136–137, 138–139, 146–147, 148, 149, 150, 151, 153, 186–87.

Jeffrey Millies for Hedrich Blessing Photographers: 8–9, 11.

Jon Miller for Hedrich Blessing Photogrphers: 82, 83.

Emily Minton: 166–167, 168, 169, 182, 183.

Ira Montgomery: 145.

Alise O'Brien: 15, 61, 62, 63, 75, 78, 79, 184.

Betty Lou Phillips: 122, 123.

Dan Piassick: Front cover, back cover, title page, 6–7, 12–13, 20, 21, 22, 23, 24, 25, 26, 27, 28, 30–31, 32–33, 34, 35, 36–37, 38, 39, 40, 41, 42, 43, 44–45, 46–47, 48, 49, 50–51, 52–53, 54, 55, 56–57, 58, 60, 64, 65, 70, 71, 84–85, 86–87, 88–89, 90, 91, 94–95, 96, 98–99, 100–101, 102, 103, 104, 105, 106, 107, 110, 111, 112, 113, 115, 116–117, 118, 119, 120, 121, 140, 141, 142, 143, 154, 155, 156, 157, 158–159, 160, 161, 162, 163, 164, 170–171, 172, 174, 176–177, 178, 181, 185.

Kenton Robertson: 81.

James F. Wilson: 144.

Page 186—87: Vaulted arches and stucco walls pay tribute to the home's Italian heritage in a hall where doors open to the pool and courtyard.